Growing Up Yesterday

These are recollections of an Italian woman in the process of growing up from an unusual childhood. The uneasy time in Mussolini's Italy and her marriage to an Englishman in the completely different atmosphere of post-war England.

GROWING
UP
YESTERDAY

by

CLEMENTINA OWLES

Illustrations by

DONALD SMITH

Regency Press (London & New York) Ltd
125 High Holborn, London WC1V 6QA

ISBN 0 7212 0692 1

Printed in Great Britain

To Nanda—who made it possible—in gratitude and to my son Francis for whom it has been written

CONTENTS

LIST OF ILLUSTRATIONS

The cover picture is of our villa and the surrounding countryside.

Growing Up Yesterday

Chapter One

CHILDHOOD

My earlier memories are of myself as a very small girl, four or five perhaps, walking down a corridor, hands firmly clasped behind my back. I wore a pale blue smock, white socks and a pair of red plimsoles with a strap across the foot and a button at one side. The corridor, which had a huge vaulted ceiling, led to the servants rooms of our country-house, Villa delle Valli.

The villa looked like a big fairy castle and was surrounded by a large park. It was in a lovely position, enjoying the view, as its name suggests, of four valleys and it was in Brianza, the beautiful countryside north of Milan in Italy.

Gentle slopes stretched down to the lakes of Como and Maggiore with small villages scattered in the valleys and at the top of the hills. The churches, in the large piazzas, were often several centuries old and here on Sundays the villagers, dressed in their best clothes, used to gather after mass and exchange the latest gossip. I remember the peal of the church bells, a soft and haunting sound, to me quite unlike all other church bells in Italy. These villages were then peaceful and rural communities very different from the semi-industrial towns they have become today.

The year must have been 1932. I would often wander into those rooms where the maids sewed and pressed. I remember the ever present smell of the scorched linen cover of the ironing board. A maid would be singing a popular song about a sick child who had been given many toys but not enough love by her mother and now she was dying and it was too late, and her mother could not make it up to her . . . overcome by the sadness of the story often I would run crying into the arms of my nurse, La Tata as everybody called her, although her name was Maria. She was a large, round, smiling woman still wearing the costume of the women of Lombardy with golden pins in her hair. I loved her and I loved pressing myself against her large bosom: I can still remember her smell of soap mixed with perspiration. She had been my wet nurse and she was the one who could best cheer me up when I felt sad or reason with me during one of my tantrums. She would sit by me when I was ill and tell me the most enchanting stories. They were all about poor or lonely children who, with the help of the Madonna or one of the saints, would eventually make good in life. Invariably with La Tata, good conquered evil and all her stories had happy endings and I would fall asleep contentedly, my childish sense of fairness completely satisfied.

I also had a nanny, a Swiss-German woman, La Fraulein, who was very strict and stern and used to pinch me blue, I swear, when I was naughty.

She always followed up her many instructions to me with *schnell* (quickly) and her stories were always about naughty children being taken away by the wolf or subjected to other well-deserved punishments which often scared me to tears.

The nursery was on the second floor of the villa and there La Fraulein reigned supreme. That was a great pity because I liked the nursery very much and I felt secure and cosy in it. It was very cheerfully decorated with bright flowers on the walls and had a huge doll's house almost as tall as myself, a cupboard filled with all sorts of stuffed animals and a rocking-horse near the window. But no sooner had I reached the top of the stairs and passed through the wooden gate which was supposed to prevent me falling down the twisting flights of stairs than La Fraulein would say, "Take off your coat and wash your hands, *schnell*", and order me about without leaving me alone for a moment. Very often she would make me eat brains and spinach because she said they would make me strong. I didn't like either of them and the brains would make me feel sick. "Please, Fraulein," I would often beg her, "May I leave them on my plate?"

"Eat up your food quickly," she would answer and, taking the fork out of my hand, she would feed me, half choking me by putting the fork too far down into my mouth. I detested her and I would whirl round and round the nursery saying louder and louder, "Horrid, horrid Fraulein, ache of my heart," (a phrase which I had picked up from one of the maids) until my head would spin and I would fall down on the floor, exhausted.

Beautifully kept grass, flowers everywhere, huge pink roses, horse-chestnut trees, and ponies in the stables. Specks of dust dancing in a sunray coming through a window, an ink-pot made out of a horse's hoof, eating red berries from the yew trees, lying flat under a tree looking through its branches at the pale blue sky. I remember the smell of the little camomile daisies in the meadows, of pine-needles which I used to chew, of the violets underneath the cedar tree.

I remember the big old family car and the many times I would be sitting next to my father at the wheel, and he would let the car roll gently down the drive to the front gate and smiling down at me he would say, "Look, I'm driving with no hands."

My parents and I spent the summer and autumn months there. I was an only child, pampered and spoiled by my parents and a great number of servants. A little girl with very fair hair and large melancholic eyes, the colour of autumn leaves I would be told later, delicate and frail, who had been given the name of her beautiful and eccentric grandmother, Clementina. My parents had lost a son, years before my arrival, and perhaps because of this tragic occurrence, they tended to over-protect me.

My mother, for instance, didn't like to have pets around the house as she believed that cats and dogs carried bugs and viruses which could give me horrible diseases.

But it was about that time that I first remember being aware of an animal. As my first encounter with a kitten was really the first memorable event in my life and also my first sorrow, I remember clearly everything connected with him.

I had discovered him during one of my walks in our park with La Tata, who was following me around, as she always did, walking slowly and knitting something with big wooden needles and a ball of wool concealed in the large pouch of her white apron. I was running about making a posy of wild flowers. It looked pretty and La Tata said that we would offer it later to the Madonna whose statue occupied a little niche at the corner of a path which led to the village. Suddenly my attention was caught by a noise which seemed to come from under a holly bush a few yards from where I was standing. There, half hidden by its leaves was a tiny kitten. It looked like one I had seen in one of those picture books with the pages made of cloth, as they used to make many years ago, a little tabby covered in mud, but real and alive! I was so thrilled about my discovery that I squatted near it to have a better look. It was very small and skinny with half-opened runny eyes. I picked him up and carrying him awkwardly in my arms, I ran back to show him to La Tata.

"Please, please," I asked her, "May I take him home with us and keep him?" She looked at him for a moment and then she said that he was certainly in need of some care and that we could talk Cook into feeding him. "But, what about the Fraulein?" she added. We walked quickly back towards the villa and through the back door and found Anna, our cook, sitting near the kitchen table, drinking coffee. "Mamma mia," she cried, "What have you got there? Poor thing, a little kitten!" She had a good look at him and declared that he was full of fleas but she warmed some milk and started to coax him into drinking it. But soon we heard the heavy and steady steps of La Fraulein coming towards us. She caught sight of the kitten and stopping half-way through a sentence she backed a few steps. Later I discovered that she was allergic to cats but, in any case, she said one shouldn't keep a dirty little thing like that in the kitchen. 'Away, away with him," she repeated, and taking me by the hand she dragged me up to the nursery to wash.

That night I couldn't sleep for the excitement and the uncertainty of the fate of the kitten but next day, after a lot of pleading with my mother, I persuaded her, with my father's help, to let me keep the kitten with us. I called him Pisolo (Sleepy) because he slept a great deal. For weeks I busied myself with him taking him to the vet with La Tata, getting him a basket where he could curl up and go to sleep, helping the cook to prepare his food. He lived mostly in the kitchen where, in the evening, he liked to sit by the fire. Anna, our cook, had taken a great liking to him. She was married to Giuseppe, the manservant, a strapping great man with a head of red hair and a skin full of freckles. He was also very quick-tempered and my mother said that he proved the saying about people with *pel di carota* (carrot hair) being bad-tempered. They lived in a cottage near the village and had a daughter, Carla, who was older than I but who often came up to the villa to help her mother and play with me. Anna made the most delicious food, which I sampled from time to time, to be sent to the dining-room. No brains and spinach were ever sent there! There was an enormous fireplace of large grey stone which took up one wall of her kitchen and often Anna would make polenta (a kind of porridge made with maze flour and cooked in a copper pot over the fire) which I was made to eat with milk while the grown-ups ate it with game or sausages.

It was because of Pisolo that Anna had a row with La Fraulein. My nanny was always complaining about him, insisting that he still had fleas (which was true) in spite of our protests that he had got rid of them with the powder the vet had given us. Once she went as far as to say that people who kept animals in their kitchen were dirty. This gave grave offence to the cook who answered her back with the most unflattering remarks about *i cruchi* (sauerkraut). It also prompted Giuseppe, a few days later, to play a shabby joke on La Fraulein.

Knowing how much she hated the touch of a cat, he waited for her to enter the store-room in which tins, cans and jars of home-made jams were kept neatly arranged on the shelves. Pushing the cat after her, he quickly closed the door behind the pair of them. To add insult to injury, he then went back to his pantry singing aloud "Vendetta, tremenda vendetta" (vengeance, dreadful vengeance), from one of Verdi's operas, I believe. He then put on his white gloves to be ready to serve us tea.

My mother and I were in the drawing-room where she was entertaining some ladies to tea. On such occasions La Fraulein would get hold of me, scrub my face and hands, comb my hair and send me to greet the guests demurely making a little curtsy to each of them. In turn they would compliment my mother saying for example: 'What a lovely child!" "Isn't she sweet?" or something of the kind which I thought was silly. If they asked me whether I had been good, my mother would invariably answer that I was a difficult child and such a worry to her, which I of course resented as being too unfair. So I hated these performances but this time we hardly had time to go through with them when we heard a series of almost inhuman cries coming from the servants' quarters. At the same time, the door of the drawing-room opened and Giuseppe appeared, looking quite unperturbed, carrying a tray with the tea things on it.

In the confusion which followed I remember quickly sneaking away but not before helping myself to some chocolate-drops which were nicely arranged in a silver box. Then I ran towards the yelling. Eventually they got the semi-conscious Fraulein out of the store-room and the uproar subsided. In what seemed to me and La Tata like a miracle, but was in fact Papa's Solomonic assertion that I shouldn't be punished for something that, I hadn't done, the cat was allowed to stay with us.

But one day I fell ill with chicken-pox and was confined to bed. I can't remember exactly when it was but Pisolo must have been by then well over a year old. I was longing to see him but the nursery was strictly 'verboten' to him and no matter how much I pleaded with mother, no matter how many tantrums I made, the veto stood. I was in despair. So, one evening when my parents were having dinner with some guests and everybody was busy in the kitchen, I got out of bed and barefoot I quietly went down the staircase and found Pisolo in the pantry. I quickly picked him up and then paused listening attentively. The door to the dining-room was open and the talking of the guests became louder. I ran back up the stairs, my heart racing, and jumped into bed hiding him with me under the sheets and blankets. He settled down purring delightedly and that night I went to sleep immensely happy, feeling his soft fur against my feverish body.

I was woken up in the morning by a shout and, slowly opening my eyes, I saw La Fraulein struggling with Pisolo who was furiously hissing at her. One of her hands was badly scratched. Then to my horror, I saw her open the window and throw the cat out. I got out of bed and ran to the window in a vain attempt to stop her.

Moments later I was looking down at the lawn where Pisolo was picking himself up with an air of bewilderment. Then I saw Carla, the cook's daughter, running towards him. She picked him up very gently and carrying him in her arms, slowly walked away towards her house. I never had him back.

Looking back, the loss of Pisolo stands out as the only dark spot in an otherwise happy memory of those early years in the countryside: blue skies only occasionally clouded by the presence of the horrid Fraulein.

Of our house in Milan, I remember the tiles of the roofs covered with snow, boxes of marrons glacés with sugar-coated violets, my great-aunt Elena bringing me small animals made of cloth, big drawing-rooms full of glittering things which I wasn't allowed to touch, a life-size painting of my grandmother on the wall, the large dining-table with a green cloth on it and again the laughter of my nurse.

I remember my little friend Carlo, the son of our neighbours. They lived in a handsome house built around a large courtyard where we children used to play. There was a well in the centre, made of stone and wrought-iron, and marble statues all around. Carlo was a little older than I and was only interested in war games. "Let's play at war," he would say distributing all his tin soldiers and toy guns behind the statues and mine around the well. His father was a general who had fought during the First World War and his tin soldiers were Italian whilst those he gave to me were Austrian, the hated enemy. Inevitably his Italian regiments would surround my troops and I had to surrender lowering my flag. Perhaps because of my docility in letting him win every battle, he was very fond of me. Once he made our parents laugh by saying to me, "Mi piaci tanto che ti mangerei in insalata" (I like you so much that I would eat you with my salad). Early signs of male possessiveness in a six-year-old!

La Fraulein still ruled my life but she was much better tempered during the months we spent in town because, as she told my mother, she was a city girl, and when she was really in a good mood she even called me darling. But I still detested her especially when she took me for walks to the public gardens and not to the park which was much nearer our house and where I had some little friends to play with.

She would sit in a shelter talking to a Swiss young man in their own language which I couldn't understand, often giggling and laughing together in the most silly way. Once I saw her crying and that really puzzled me as I couldn't believe that nannies could ever cry. "Run along and go and play with the other children . . . schnell!" she would tell me but I didn't know any of them and I was shy and it was very cold and my nose was dripping and my feet were frozen. "Horrid, horrid Fraulein," I would say to myself as I walked away from them, dragging my feet in the gravel and watching my breath steaming in the air. How much I disliked those walks!

'Why does Father Christmas come down the chimney?" "Why was the Child Jesus born in a manger?" "Why was He so poor if He was the Son of God?" "Why, why . . .?" So many questions, so many puzzles and rarely the grown-ups would come up with a satisfactory answer. But Christmas was definitely fun, the shepherds would come and play their lovely songs on their bagpipes outside the front door and the streets were all covered with snow; many small children were invited to the house to play with me and we were given a smashing tea. My hair was all done up in little curls and I was wearing a pretty new dress.

The Christmas tree was brought into the drawing-room in great secret and decorated by my mother after I had gone to sleep. The next morning I would look, spellbound and dazzled, at all the lovely many-coloured decorations which were glittering gaily from its branches.

A great number of parcels were piled up at the foot of the huge fir-tree, one for each member of the household and, perhaps, more than one for me if I had been good.

"Is Giuseppe going to receive his present?" I asked knowing that he hadn't been good at all because La Tata had said that he had made Cook cry. Yes, he was. "Why then . . .?" But like so many other whys, this one too was to remain without an answer.

But then the picture changes in my memory. I see my mother crying, my father looking gloomy and dismal, my nurse packing her bags in her room, blowing her nose into her handkerchief, the other servants whispering among themselves, food left uneaten on the plates of my parents. I remember being told to be especially quiet, because my father was very sick, and running to his room and finding the door locked from the inside. He had lost a great part of what he owned, which was indeed quite considerable.

I was never told exactly what happened, nor what caused him to be almost ruined. My parents never spoke about it to me. Years later I overheard my mother telling the story to a friend implying that wrong speculations had been made and mentioning the name of a man who had badly cheated him.

Gone was the pink villa towering above the valleys where I was born and my father and my grandfather before me and, with it, the stables, the estate, the house in town, the trips abroad, the lavish parties, the servants and . . . some friends. As my father would say, we had suddenly become *nouveaux pauvres!*

I remember my father very well. As a child I worshipped him and I was full of admiration for everything he said and did. He was very handsome, tall with grey-green eyes and receding fair hair which he nonetheless brushed well back from the forehead. His hands were particularly beautiful with long tapering fingers and well manicured finger-nails.

He was a very cultured man with a delicious sense of humour and a sense of fun which made him imitate everyone's accent and mannerism in three different languages. To amuse me and my little friends around the dining-table, he would often make fun of everything which had happened to him, good or bad, often relating the event in a distorted and exaggerated way. Quite often it was sheer nonsense and my mother, who didn't like fun for fun's sake and was always preoccupied with setting a good example to us children, would listen to him silent and tense, not a shade of a smile crossing her face. But, of course, we children loved the performance and roared with laughter. At other times if my mother happened to mention casually that she had just met a Mrs. X, father would suddenly become a silly, fat, middle-aged woman discussing her rheumatism and sciatica, hobbling around the room with a stiff leg and a hand behind his back. Mother would then say to him, in her prim way, that he was a cause of embarrassment to her because of his habit of making fun of the most serious situations. Suddenly Mrs. X would disappear and her place would be taken by a very repentant man who was overwhelmed by remorse!

Daddy belonged to a very old family from the North of Italy and was an only child, a daughter having died of diphtheria seven years before he was born. His childhood and youth were spent in a rather carefree and frivolous way like those of many other people of the same social class during that period usually known as "La belle époque", from around the end of the nineteenth century to the Great War of 1914–18. But he fought in that war from which he was lucky enough to come back, minus two little toes which he lost because of frostbite. His greatest interests were history and literature and by the time of his bankruptcy in 1933, when he was forty, he had travelled widely around the world and collected a valuable library.

I remember clearly the precious times when, sitting in his armchair in front of a log fire, he would take me on his lap and lovingly would tell me about his family. He mixed a loving pride with a sense of almost unbelievable admiration for his mother when he described her to me.

Daddy's father was a country gentleman who had married late in life. Since his marriage, however, mostly to please his young wife, he had lived in a house in town escaping to his country house during the summer and autumn months. He didn't seem to have worked an hour of his life apart from instructing his 'man' to look after his estates. He was known as a kind, rather dull, easy-going man. His saving grace, in the eyes of some of his friends, was that he took along with him on his honeymoon to Paris, a ballerina from La Scala of Milan.

But there was a certain eccentricity in the family and this came, according to my mother who never stopped reminding us, from "all those Slavs" on her mother-in-law's side. It seemed to me that, most of all, they were remarkable non-conformists who were so comfortably sure of themselves and of their own background, not to worry in the least about how other people might judge them.

My grandmother Clementina had a grandfather who was a Polish count and a general who fought on the side of Russia in the Napoleonic campaign of 1812. In recognition of his gallantry and services, the Czar Alexander gave him an exact small reproduction of the column erected in his honour in the centre of the Hermitage Square in Leningrad where the original still stands. Later the general had to leave Poland for political reasons and emigrated to Italy. The small column, 1·45m. tall, went with him and it has been in the family since. I remember, as a child, seeing a picture of him, amid a battlefield, a sword in his right hand, astride a rearing horse with its hoofs up in mid-air. I imagined him galloping across Europe, followed by hordes of murderous Cossacks, holding his precious column under one arm!

Clementina was one of the most beautiful women of her time and equally capricious. Having been married at seventeen to an older man who didn't fully understand her, and who in any case much preferred the easy love of a ballerina, she settled down to play the part expected of her in the society of her time where beauty and position were of paramount importance in the life of a woman. I have always thought that this didn't really satisfy her and that her eccentricities were an outlet for her frustrations. She was wilful and independent with a passion for the arts. She must have accepted with great difficulty her arranged marriage. La bella Clementina, as she was so often called, would ride one day with the king and the next befriend her farrier. She would appear at a fancy dress ball (as an old snapshot shows) stunningly dressed in yellow and orange silks and with yards of tulle and sequins around her head to represent the sun, and then perhaps disappear into a convent for a month or so, to lead the life of a nun.

She kept a salon in which she entertained the most influential people and the young, unknown, and sometimes not very respectable, artists and intellectuals. She was careful not to mix the two but, even so, occasionally that would cause a raised eyebrow even among the most well-disposed friends. But, most of all, by all accounts, she was generous and kind, helping extravagantly anyone who knocked at her door.

Her younger sister Elena had been a spinster for many years. She had lived alone in a big rambling house in Brianza, the Manor House, surrounded by dogs and cats, smoking cigars and generally leading what to the village people, must have seemed a very liberated life. I used to go and stay with her when she was quite old and I enjoyed her informality and casualness. She was tall and slim with deep-set green eyes and an enormous quantity of perfectly white hair which she kept in a coil on the nape of her neck. In the evening, when she changed before dinner, she would allow me to go to her dressing room and help her brush her hair. It was very long and silky and when she let it fall onto her shoulders she looked to me almost ethereal, like an elf out of one of my picture-books. "Come," she would say, "Come and look at my treasure trove," and out of faded velvet boxes would emerge her trinkets, precious cameos, an old curl, fans made of fine lace and small albums in which she kept dried pansies and masses of photographs mostly of her pets but also of a man, Francesco. Apparently Francesco was an immensely charming man, a much sought-after bachelor, with a passion for horses and racing. He had met the two sisters when they were still in their teens and had fallen madly in love with Clementina, then a young bride. She fell to his charms and love but never left her husband for him. I suppose, it must have been a kind of successful *ménage à trois* because, in fact, it lasted for over thirty years. All through this time, Elena was also secretly in love with Francesco and persistently and stubbornly turned down every marriage proposal which her mother and sister hopefully put forward to her.

When Clementina died of Spanish flu' in 1918, Francesco was heart-broken and let himself be consoled by sweet Elena who managed to patch up his aching heart with loving care and lots of patience. She was nearly fifty by then and, at last, she saw an opportunity to fulfil her life-long dream: she proposed to him . . . and was accepted.

My mother entered into this family with what must have been, to say the least, mixed feelings. She came from a very solid and respectable Piedmontese family, highly religious and dedicated to good work. She was an orphan and had been brought up by an aunt and her husband, an elderly couple who died before her marriage to my father. I rarely saw any of her other relations.

She was pretty, petite, with nice features and a particularly lovely smile which she kept until old age. Hers had been a love match but in the beginning, at least, she had been repelled and fascinated at the same time by the family she had married into; they were flamboyant and gay, disrespectful of old traditions and customs. She had grown up in an atmosphere where everybody knew his place in the world and kept it and where the sense of duty was strongly felt.

At the time of their marriage my parents had considerable means and they settled down to a very pleasant life. Soon a son was born. He was breast-fed by a wet nurse who unfortunately was an alcoholic and by the time this was discovered, the baby fell sick with enteritis and died. I was born years later, when my mother was already forty-three.

I hesitate to talk about my mother because, in spite of all her good qualities, all my thoughts of her are either sad or downright sorrowful. I feel I really never understood her well and, therefore, I can't be objective about her. Not only was there more than a generation gap between our ages but also my rather non-conformist way of thinking didn't help matters. I also felt that I didn't turn out as she would have liked a daughter of hers to be and, in fact, she often said so herself. She had great courage and accepted with considerable fortitude the many trials which befell her. I admired her much for that, but I wish I could have loved her more and my greatest regret is not to have been able to do so during her long life.

Chapter Two

MONTE CARLO

In 1933 the Italian lira was a strong currency, stronger than the French franc, or so it seems, as I was told by my parents that one of the reasons for our going to live in an hotel in Monte Carlo was the favourable rate of exchange of the lira in respect to the franc. Another reason was that they wanted to get away from their recent financial troubles and plan for the future.

The hotel was at the Condamine, a district near the harbour, and it was modest, old-fashioned and reasonably cheap. It certainly didn't have the elegance and luxury of those up the ramp near the casino.

Staying at the same hotel was an American boy called Buster who, perhaps, is responsible for my instinctive liking of Americans. He had red hair and freckles and was the most mischievous little chap I ever met. He was there with his widowed mother who, for reasons better known to herself, had decided that a little hotel in Monte Carlo was a suitable place to reside with her seven-year-old son. They had been there already for some time before our arrival and the management of the hotel had more than once hinted to her that small Buster would have been far better off in a proper school, if not in an American institution for juvenile delinquents.

We were the only children there, the other guests being mainly elderly people whom Buster tried to frighten to death. He seemed to concentrate all his energy in working out plans to annoy them. He was a stocky little fellow, short and strongly limbed with narrow deep-set eyes that looked at you with an intensity more often found in snakes. One of his pet hates was an old man who used to sit every afternoon in the lounge sipping his tea. Buster would stare at him from across the room and make as to bash him on the head with the wooden pole which held the daily newspaper. He would brandish it and charge towards the poor man, often causing him to spill his tea whilst shaking with apprehension.

Another one was Mlle Duprés. She was an old spinster, small and absurdly fat, with her hair set in a frame of little yellow curls around her rather silly face. She used to take her meals in the dining room at the same time as us children, a little before the other guests. Once he put a small frog under her napkin which was resting on a plate in front of her. When Mlle Duprés, sitting down at her table, unfolded the napkin, the frog leaped on her lap and then to the floor. The poor soul sat there, speechless with shock until a waiter gave her some brandy to revive her. Buster, who was sitting at the next table, continued to drink his soup perhaps with a louder sucking noise than usual, but seeming not to pay the slightest attention to her. Later on, when told to go and apologise to mademoiselle, he went up to her and said accusingly, "Tu es si vilaine que tu as fait peur même à la grenouille!" (You are so ugly that you have frightened even the frog!)

Buster would jam the old-fashioned lift, making each ascent an adventure for the hotel guests, overflow the bath-tub and pee in the potted plants which decorated the hall and the writing room. Like so many other boys, he used to collect all sorts of insects which he kept in matchboxes in a drawer beside his bed. He would let them loose around the place, often creeping slowly behind a guest to plant a little beast on his shoulder or head.

He was quite a nasty little boy and I was completely fascinated by him. In the beginning he considered me just a silly little girl unworthy of his attention but when it dawned on him that I could be of some use to him as a more than willing accomplice, he accepted me. He expected from me "an absolute ready and blind obedience", to use his own words. He made me pledge it, solemnly and in writing, on a piece of paper which we both ceremoniously burnt. From that moment whenever I hesitated to follow his instructions to the letter, he would accuse me of being a weakling. This would generally lead to a quarrel. I would have given anything to be as imaginative and wicked as he was and I couldn't bear to be considered soft. When this happened we shouted furiously at each other in French using the polite form of *vous* rather than the usual more familiar *tu* and, when we had exhausted all the possible insults of which we were capable, we would sulk or speak to each other in our own language which the other one couldn't understand.

This kind of love/hate relationship lasted for almost a year until his mother was asked in no uncertain way to move to a more suitable place. This final crisis was provoked by the fact that Buster had hid himself in a cave near the sea *pour fair croire au monde que je suis mort* (to make everyone believe that he was dead) and, in fact, for a while he was feared to be drowned. The police were notified and a lot of time and effort were spent on a search. When he finally was found, home and dry so to speak, munching biscuits and nuts in his cave, there was a chain reaction which ended with Buster and his poor mother sailing back to the United States.

I was inconsolable. But for the guests of the hotel it was like a new lease of life and one could see those elderly people congratulating each other on their good fortune with great sighs of relief: no more insects in their beds and plates, no more dangerous lifts to their rooms, no fear of any more games of redskins lurking behind armchairs with their bows and arrows. Most of all, my mother was delighted to see the departure of such a bad influence on her already difficult little daughter.

I suppose I was difficult and this was due, especially after Buster's departure, to the fact that I was lonely and often bored. My mother's deep concern about the future and a way of life so different from the orderly way she had been brought up didn't help her to be even-tempered. The result was a sort of war of nerves in which she would swing erratically from spoiling me with treats and presents she could ill-afford, to an unreasonable severity and punishment. I never knew where I stood with her. On the other hand, I felt that daddy was always on my side and that he tried to act as a buffer between the two of us. He was really my best friend, even better than Buster!

It was in Monte Carlo that I first remember the beginning of many head-on clashes with my mother.

A lot of my parents' friends came over from Italy to visit us and have a fling at the casino. So my parents often met interesting people, played tennis and sailed despite their much reduced financial circumstances. Often they went out in the evening, and I remember them coming into my bedroom to say goodnight. They made such a handsome couple, my father resplendent in a white dinner-jacket and mother in a ruby-red long dress which enhanced her dark colouring with a black velvet cape lined with white fur on her shoulders. I can still smell her scent as she bent down to kiss me. "Sleep well," she would say, "And don't turn the light on again as you usually do, you must sleep now."

But, of course, as soon as they left, I would switch on the light above my bed partly because I was afraid of the dark and partly because I wanted to play with my stuffed animals. I would gather them all around me and often fall asleep in the middle of my play.

On morning mother must have been in a particularly bad mood because, on discovering once more that the lights were on, instead of the usual mild scolding she turned sharply on me and said crossly, "It's time you learnt how to behave and tonight I shall take the bulb away. And you shall stay in your room until I tell you." She left closing the door behind her and I heard the key turning in the lock.

"This is really the wrong day to make her cross," I thought, "But let's hope she'll remember that she has promised to take me to see the carnival." This was a beautiful parade of floats with enormous animals, clowns, pretty girls and flower decorations which rode down the main roads, the whole show culminating in a firework display. I was sitting miserably on my bed when I heard my mother calling me from the road outside. I rushed to the balcony ready to join her. She looked up at me and said something like "Naughty girl; serves you right," before leaving in company of a friend. Tears of frustration and hurt pride filled my eyes as I watched her walking briskly away from the hotel. I went slowly back into the room and looked around. On an armchair in a corner there were two fine lace cushions which she had salvaged from our house in Milan with her initials embroidered on them. With a pair of scissors, very slowly and very carefully, first I shredded to ribbons the large initials, then I made a hole in the pink silk and out came thousands of small pretty feathers. By the time my mother came back the whole room was covered with them. The punishment was swift and immediate: two quick slaps on my face and then to bed without even saying goodnight to daddy.

A few days later I got into trouble again for answering back. It had been quite a vocal match which led to a new type of punishment. I was to stay in my room without dinner. At eight-thirty I was still locked up, hungry and bored. Then I had an idea: why not get the waiter to come up with my favourite meal? (Spaghetti, veal steak with chips and ice-cream.) After all, I reasoned, he had his keys and could open any door of the hotel. I picked up the room telephone and ordered. I was just finishing a super meal when my father appeared, worried about his poor child being left starving. In a flash he took in the whole situation and roared with laughter!

It seems to me that, once mother and I had started on this collision course, there were endless occasions and possibilities for us to go on, and in fact, that's exactly what we did.

Once I got lost on the Corniche, a lovely winding road on the hills above the sea. We had gone away for the day taking a basketful of food to have a picnic in the woods. On the way back home I was running about collecting interesting pebbles when I overheard my mother and a friend of hers discussing, if you please, my frightful disobedience and my father's lack of discipline. I was indignant and began to walk behind them slower and slower until they reached a crossroad and turned left. I turned right. I had no clear idea of where I was going, the only important thing was to be as far away as possible from my mother. So I kept walking in the opposite direction to where the voice was calling me. It was becoming quite dark and I was beginning to feel tired and a little afraid but I kept plodding along. Eventually the path led me back to Monte Carlo where I took a pony and trap to the hotel and asked the hall porter to pay for the ride.

I went through the hall amid cries of "Voilà la petite demoiselle,"—"La voilà," "Où est sa pauvre maman?" etc.

My *pauvre maman* was lying on her bed with *une migraine* and I got one of the very rare beatings, if not the only one, my father ever gave me in all my life.

Living in an hotel full of elderly people wasn't the ideal thing for a little girl but soon the arrival of the new guest brought some fun into my life in the shape of a dog. I don't think I ever knew the owner's surname as everybody called her Madame la Comtesse but her first name was Natasha. As a matter of fact, she wasn't new at all because she had stayed at the hotel, on and off, many times before, but she had been away when we first got there. She was a White Russian, tall and slim, she held herself very straight. She must have been around forty. Her face was pale and the white

Madame la Comtesse

make-up she always wore contrasted strongly with the scarlet of her lips and the black of her eyes and hair. I thought she was immensely elegant. But if I was fascinated by her, I was bowled over by her dog. He was a slender, absolutely magnificent greyhound with thin, long legs which seemed perpetually trembling with excitement. She called him Golubchik which is Russian for "my little pigeon, my darling", and he was the only dog in the hotel. His real name was Vladimir.

The reason why Natasha and her greyhound found themselves in our modest hotel must have been the lack of funds necessary to keep them in the style to which they had been accustomed in old Russia. Perhaps the sharing of financial difficulties and the poor choice of the other guests of the hotel encouraged the friendship which soon grew between her and my parents. They were often joined by an elderly Frenchman, Monsieur Duval, and the four of them, with Vladimir and me leading the way, could often be seen walking up and down the promenade.

Monsieur Duval was an insignificant little man, fat and bald and with thick glasses. He was a retired businessman from Lyons and a widower and he had come, originally, to spend two weeks in Monte Carlo but was still there, months later, smitten by Madame la Comtesse. He would look at her with an adoring expression on his silly face. A most ridiculous expression, I thought, like that of a dead fish.

For her sake, although he didn't much care for dogs, he made great efforts to be friendly with Vladimir who for some reason, had taken a great dislike to him, once or twice even biting his hand while the poor man tried to pat him. But Monsieur Duval was besotten with Natasha and proposed marriage to her only to be turned down with a laugh. "Never, never would I consent to be married to such a boring little man," she would say to my mother during one of their talks in which Natasha would pour her heart out and discuss the difficulties she had to face, the lack of money and the lack of social graces of Monsieur Duval.

She was a very temperamental woman and suffered from frequent changes of mood. My father, who was very much under her spell, would find excuses for such behaviour but mother would sharply comment on it and suggest that she should be sensible and be nice to Monsieur Duval. But Natasha didn't want to be sensible and she would pawn one of her jewels and gamble at the casino.

Gambling, of course, was the fashionable thing to do in Monte Carlo. My father would sometimes escort Madame la Comtesse to the casino to play chemin de fer but mother and Monsieur Duval would remain at the hotel because they strongly disapproved of any form of gambling.

Often Natasha would allow me to take Vladimir for walks on a beautiful red leash of crocodile leather and I enjoyed these outings very much. Once we had gone up towards the gardens near the pink and white palace where the Princes of Monaco lived. Vladimir was walking by me, sniffing here and there, and lifting his elegant leg against various benches which he obviously thought were put there especially for him. A dog was coming from the opposite direction. She was a small grey poodle, beautifully groomed, with a collar studded with pretty stones, and she was trailing her lead. Vladimir was electrified at this sight and pulling away from me, ran towards her on his swift, long legs.

What happened next was a mystery in my innocent eyes and I watched with great interest Vladimir's extraordinary behaviour.

After a while I heard a voice calling "Nanette, Nanette, come here, come to your maman," and a middle-aged woman, out of breath and flushed in the face, walked quickly towards us. When she saw the dogs together she became very cross and tried to divide them, talking fast all the time and accusing me of not being able to control my dog. Finally she managed to pick up Nanette and carry her away under her arm. I could still hear her scolding the little bitch long after they had disappeared from my sight.

Vladimir and I went back to the hotel where I told Natasha what had happened wondering whether she would also be cross with me. But she only laughed. "The silly woman," she said, "I know her and I shall send her some flowers in three months' time! That was Golubchik having a bit of fun. That's how puppies are made, darling, don't you know?" More interesting explanations followed. Unfortunately the arrival of my mother put a stop to them because she quickly changed the conversation and sent me up to her room to fetch her shawl.

One day daddy and I had just come back from the beach and we were getting ready for luncheon when Natasha, looking very upset and red-eyed, asked to have a word with daddy. It transpired that she had run out of jewels to pawn and that she was behind with the payment of her hotel bill. The management had written to her saying that as she had been staying with them for such a long time, they would allow her to stay on a while longer (after all Madame la Comtesse was a good advertisement for the place and in the past she had brought in many other émigré friends) but Vladimir had to go. Apparently they had received many complaints from the other guests about her dog.

Natasha was in despair. "How could I part from him?" she was now saying dramatically. "Would you want me to get rid of my only child? Never, never would I part from Golubchik, no matter what happens."

A few days later I was called to the hall of the hotel to say goodbye to Natasha. She stood near the entrance door looking very beautiful in a pink dress and a hat made of pink feathers. All the hotel staff were there standing in a line to say goodbye to her. The manager came and kissed her hand and the hall porter, in black tails with two golden keys on each lapel of his coat, had tears in his eyes. Then mountains of luggage were brought down from her room—trunks, suitcases and hat boxes.

Natasha went through the revolving door with Vladimir at her heels. Outside, in the brilliant sunshine, stood an open car with

Monsieur Duval at the wheel. The porter opened the door for her and she sat next to him. Vladimir jumped on the back seat. Slowly they drove off toward Menton and the Italian border.

"Poor Monsieur Duval," said daddy who had also come out to wish her *bon vóyage.* "It will not be easy for him, what with one thing and another and Vladimir to top it all!"

So that was goodbye to Vladimir but shortly after that, my father took my education into his hands and got from Italy all the textbooks needed to coach me in what should have been my first year of elementary school. Every day we worked together and he taught me how to read and write in Italian and French. I took to reading like a duck to water, at first slowly and aloud to anyone who cared to listen, and then to myself reading beginners' books where the words were written in large letters and only a few in each page and with lovely pictures of animals in them. And that was exciting because the Piglet, the Goose and all the rest of them became real to me and I would talk to them continuously as if they were real people.

Later, of course, I graduated to bigger books and Aunt Elena sent me Hans Christian Andersen's *Fairy Tales* with the dedication: "To darling Clementina who had discovered the pleasures of reading—may her life be full of books!" But the book wasn't a success. With daddy's help, I plunged into it but my eyes would fill up with tears more often than not. The first tale in the book was the one about the fir-tree which was taken from its beautiful forest to be put in a drawing room as a Christmas tree and it ended (after Christmas was over): "The servant came and cut the tree into small pieces; heaped them up, and set fire to them. And the tree groaned, and every groan sounded like a little explosion . . ." Poor little tree! And then, of course, there was *The Little Match-girl* who was found frozen to death on the last night of the old year. And the little girl Karen in *The Red Shoes* whose heart was so full of sunshine, of peace and gladness, that it broke. Not to mention *The Little Mermaid* and her unhappy love for the prince.

But in spite of this bad start, I retained a great love for books and reading filled up many lonely hours of my life with pleasure and excitement.

Being coached by daddy didn't really take up much of our time and during the long summer on the Riviera I used to go for long walks on the beaches until I was so tired that I would lie face down on the sand and watch the little crabs walk sideways and disappear into a hole. I knew as yet nothing of beauty but the sea fascinated me and as I learned to swim on the lovely shores of the Mediterranean I began my long love affair with the sea.

I must have had too much of a good thing because once I had sunstroke. I remember lying in bed, my room quite dark because the shutters had been pulled down to keep all the sunlight out, and sinking into a world of make-believe.

I was in a cave full of little people down near the place where the rocks touched the sea and they all looked beautiful and happy and they had a lot of small animals around them. I wanted to live with them but they said that I could only stay if my eyes were blue. "Please may I have blue eyes?" I asked mother who was sitting on a chair near my bed, "They won't have me if I haven't got blue eyes."

"Who are they?" mother wanted to know.

"The elfs and the fairies, of course."

"You have too much imagination, be still and try to go to sleep."

"What is imagination?"

"It means seeing things differently to how they are. It means making things up, and that is naughty."

"But I can see them quite well exactly as they are. I have no imagination!" I was cross now, why couldn't she ever believe me? "Be still," she repeated putting her cool hand on my forehead, "You have a temperature."

"If I go to sleep will God change my eyes for me?" I asked.

How well I remember this piece of conversation and my frustration for not being believed! Later the doctor came and said I had sunstroke: "You must wear a hat when you sit in the sun," he ordered before going away.

A hat in the sun . . . a hat in the sun . . . but I shall wear a crown of flowers like the Queen Elf . . . I fell asleep.

The next two days I was still tired and had a headache and was kept in bed. The doctor came back a few days later and examined me. He pulled down my lower eyelid and looked carefully at the white of the eye and said that I was anaemic. He prescribed some cod-liver oil capsules and told me to eat a lot of liver and spinach. "Perhaps you could drink a little red wine," he added giving me a wink.

And so from that day on I was given half a glass of wine diluted with water with my meals for the rest of the time we spent in Monte Carlo.

I soon got better and was allowed back to the beach and made to wear a white cotton hat which was put wet on my head. We lived at the hotel a little while longer but clouds were gathering near the Horn of Africa and soon the Abyssinian war put an end to our stay there.

Chapter Three

MILAN

In 1935 Italy invaded Abyssinia. For a while the expansionist Fascist régime had been looking around for a suitable place to build its empire. A border clash between Ethiopia and Italian Somaliland gave Mussolini the pretext to go to war.

When the news of the Italian build-up of troops was splashed in the newspapers all around the world, my father, restless in Monte Carlo, welcomed the African adventure as a way of escaping the boredom of his present life and promptly joined up. He resented his present financial condition which was so different from that of all his friends and, being an intellectual, he tended to be socially isolated, self-conscious and over-civilised. War offered him an escape from his personal problems, a release from social bonds, a situation in which the primitive instincts of aggression and self-sacrifice were approved and encouraged.

He was then forty-two. He was given a commission and together with his men he sailed from Naples to East Africa. We were all sure he would come back triumphant at the end of the war, like Aida's Vincitore, to the sound of the *coro trionfale*.

During the period that my father was away in Abyssinia, my mother and I lived in a small hotel in Milan. The place was run by two middle-aged lesbians. The elder, Maria, was a spinster, tall and stout with the beginning of a moustache and big, dark circles under her black eyes. The other, Giulia, had been married but had left her husband and gone to live with her friend. They were well-born and well-educated women but because of their situation they led a lonely and isolated life. With the help of a cook and a maid they looked after their guests, mostly impoverished and elderly gentlefolk who might not have had a hint of the relationship between them, were it not for the continuous quarrels between the two. As it was, because of the cheap rates charged and the genteel old-world atmosphere of the place, they pretended to ignore it, the old boys even making discrete advances to them.

Once a proffered rose caused a terrible scene of jealousy which I witnessed by chance. I happened to walk into a room and saw Maria and Giulia rolling on the floor hitting each other with such gusto that I stood there spellbound watching them tear themselves apart.

Towards the end of our stay Maria went on a crash slimming course consisting of taking very hot baths and swallowing great quantities of vinegar. As her weight went down her rows with Giulia multiplied, and her nerves gave way to exhaustion.

One day she died of a massive heart attack. This was my first contact with death. I remember sneaking unnoticed into her room and with a feeling of incredulity and horror I saw her lying dead on her bed, a rosary in her hands, with that unbelievable stillness and that awful colour on her face.

Her death made a great impression on me and for nights afterwards I dreamt of her rising from her deathbed, slowly coming towards me and trying to touch me with her icy hands. Reliving in my sleep the scenes I had witnessed between her and Giulia, I would substitute myself for her companion and, pushing her away from me, I would try to yell at her, "Maria, you are old, old, you make me sick! "But my voice wouldn't come out of me and Maria would come closer and closer. "How beautiful you are," she would whisper to me with her lips bluish and livid, "Let me touch you," and I would wake up and scream in terror.

I had begun to attend school, which was a short walk away from our hotel. Mother would take me there every morning and we would stop on our way at the bar at the corner of our road and drink a *caffelatte* (coffee with a lot of milk) and eat a croissant. The barman at the counter, a big burly chap, would hand me the warm croissant with a big grin. "Ah, ecco la principessina," he would say, "Shall we put some.pink back into her cheeks?" And he would squeeze my cheek hard between his two fat hairy fingers. How annoying that was! But I was too shy to remonstrate.

Often in winter the streets were thick with fog and mother would tell me to keep my mouth firmly shut so that it wouldn't go down to my lungs and make them all black. It was also very cold and I was covered with layers and layers of clothes which made me feel all stiff and uncomfortable. But school was all right. For one thing, daddy had done his tutoring very well and I wasn't behind the other girls in any subject and very much better at reading and writing, but, most of all, it was very nice to be with other children. I remember being teased a lot in the beginning, but I don't quite recall why. Perhaps it was because mother dressed me in a rather old-fashioned way and my skirts were a lot longer than the average, or perhaps, because after more than two years of speaking French in Monte Carlo I had a slight accent in Italian, or simply because I was an only child and unlike them. However, it couldn't have been very bad because I mostly remember my pleasure in going to school. From the first day I was asked to sit in the front row of the desks next to Annetta, an irrepressible brunette with an infectious laugh, who soon became my bosom friend.

As lessons were only in the morning as in most other schools in Italy, I would often be invited to spend the afternoon at her house. We would have little homework to do but Annetta often had lines to copy out because she was a great chatterbox. As I could write so much faster than she, I would generally copy them out for her. I must say that I didn't do her work because I was particularly kind or because I wanted to show off, but simply because we would have more time to play with all her wonderful toys and I never had enough of playing. I always played in dead earnest. Annetta was the youngest of the family and the cupboard and shelves of her bedroom were full of boxes of puzzles and games and tattered dolls and fluffy animals (often without an eye or an ear) mostly handed down to her by her elder sisters. There was a lot of laughter at her house. They all seemed so happy and good-tempered and even her nanny was nice and easy-going and fat. Funny that . . . I remember being surprised because all the nannies I knew were very thin. I discussed this fact with Annetta who said that her father only employed fat women because they were much jollier and cosier.

Instead I was rather thin and becoming a delicate, over-sensitive child never far away from tears. "Hai le lacrime in tasca" ("You have tears in your pockets") my mother used to say, "Aren't you ashamed of yourself?"

I hated my days at the hotel, dull and lonely. I hated the depressive atmosphere of the place, the look of the other guests and their continuous petty squabbling, the long dark corridors, the dirty and smelly dining room, the over-worked maid who went about the place in slippers, her grey-coloured stockings twisting and folding around her legs. I hated being taken to the zoo and to the circus to look at those poor animals kept in their narrow cages or at the clowns hitting each other on the head: they all looked so very sad to me.

But my tears turned to laughter watching the films of Laurel and Hardy which were dubbed into Italian with a strong English accent making them sound even funnier and I would roll with laughter in my seat at their comic pranks.

And, most of all, there were Charlie Chaplin's films. Going to see them was really the highlight of that period because I was completely fascinated by the little tramp and although I didn't as yet understand the satire and the melodrama of his films, the slapstick and the fantasy in them held me spellbound.

I would be taken by mother to see them and then again by Aunt Elena who loved them almost as much as I did, and when La Tata came to town to visit us, always bringing with her a large basket full of fresh eggs and freshly baked cakes, I would beg her to accompany me. Somehow she didn't seem to enjoy them very much because often she would fall asleep in her seat and snore gently all through the performance. But she would sit up straight and listen carefully during the showing of the news reel which was mostly about the Abyssinian war and the comings and goings of Mussolini.

She approved of him because he had made peace with the Pope. (She meant the Lateran Treaty, the 1929 Concordat between the Holy See and the Italian Government that restored the temporal sovereignty of the Pope and the rights of the Church in Italy which were suspended in 1870 after the seizure of the Papal States by Italy.) Also because he had been a socialist like her dead husband. "He comes from the working class, like us," she would say. "E poi è bello" (and then he is handsome). And that always seemed to end the argument!

And so, between laughter and tears and clashes with my mother, those two years passed by and daddy came back from Africa.

Mother and I went down to Naples to meet his boat and the

quay was full of people waving the Italian flag and singing *Faccetta Nera* (a popular song about Little Black Face going to be much happier now that she had another Duce and another King!). Father, in his khaki uniform, looked well and sun-tanned and had some new medals pinned on his chest. My heart swelled with pride and admiration, but no sooner had he hugged and kissed us than these feelings of mine were shattered by his contemptuously saying that the whole thing had been nothing but bloody tomfoolery!

However as the problem to find some remunerative work was still there, in spite of having helped conquer Ethiopia and make his king an emperor, he resolved it by going back to the services and joined the Italian Air Force in Libya.

Before daddy left for Libya, in fact shortly after his return from Ethiopia, it was decided that I should be prepared for my first communion. This, as we all know, is an event of the greatest importance and solemnity in the Catholic religion. Heated arguments which reached enormous proportions and involved also a priest and some nuns, took place between mother and myself on the subject of religion.

Like the great majority of Italians I was born into a Roman Catholic family. Mother was a very devout and staunch member of the Church, for ever attending services and asking special grace in return for so many rosaries and other penances. Father kept an open mind, which meant a policy of non-interference with the business of God. He had talked to me about many things and taught me history and poetry, the love of books and the appreciation of beauty but had never discussed religion with me.

Before being sent to learn the catechism, my formal religious education consisted mainly in saying a few prayers before going to sleep asking the child Jesus to make me good, and in going to Mass with mother and behaving myself during the service. It meant sitting quietly and kneeling at the right moment without turning my head around or putting my finger in my nose, a thing I was inclined to do when bored.

My nurse had often talked to me about the Madonna, the Holy Virgin, whose statuette, prettily dressed in a pale blue garment and with a halo around her head, lived in a little niche at the corner of two roads just outside the garden walls of our former country house. During our walks in the park my nurse would help me make a little posy of wild flowers which we would offer to her. This Madonna was thought to be particularly miraculous and, in fact, she was surrounded by many silver hearts offerings given by people in gratitude for graces received through her.

Once I had asked her to make me find a puppy in the nursery on returning from my walk but, although I felt pretty sure that she would answer my prayers after all those bunches of flowers I had gathered for her, there was no puppy waiting for me when I expectantly ran up the stairs to my room.

Now, as part of my spiritual preparation, I was sent to the nearby convent to be taught catechism about the dogmas and the mysteries of the Catholic Church.

I arrived accompanied by my mother who left me in the care of a nun urging me to behave myself. "Fa la brava, Clementina, fa la brava" (Promise me to be good, Clementina) said in such a doubtful tone of voice as if she felt some premonition of trouble ahead.

There were some other little girls standing around in the courtyard all waiting for the arrival of the priest. Not knowing anybody there I sat in a corner, feeling very shy, for what seemed a long time. Then one of the girls came over to me. She was older than I and had an air of a little-know-all about her. She asked me whether I knew about the miracle of the wafer which was really the body of Christ. Was I ready *to eat* Him for the first time soon? "Certainly not," I replied very much taken aback, "And I don't believe you anyway! Why should he want to be eaten by me?" All the other girls who had been listening to our conversation began to giggle confirming my idea that she was just pulling my leg.

Unfortunately, in spite of weeks of instructions, coaxing and scolding by the good priest, some nuns and my mother, I wouldn't change my mind and every time I was asked by one of them: "Do you believe in the mystery of the wafer?" I would silently shake my head.

Then an old nun told us a story which scared me out of my wits. It was about the Devil, who lived in the house of an unbeliever in the shape of a monkey, and the holy water which eventually defeated him. The story was about Don Mario, a priest, and his childhood friend Antonio, a young vet who unfortunately became an atheist. In spite of their different beliefs, the two still remained friends. The vet lived near the church and often Don Mario would spend an evening with him in the hope, perhaps, of eventually converting his wayward friend. One day Antonio acquired a little monkey which had been taken to his surgery in need of some care and he had brought her to his flat. She was unusually clever and intelligent and soon became very attached to him. She had learned to do a few things around the house like opening doors and welcoming her master's visitors but she seemed to dislike Don Mario intensely. Every time he came to the house and when she would happen to open the door, she would shriek in anger at his sight and run away from him. At other times she would throw herself at him, even creeping under his long black gown in an effort to bite at his ankles. The two friends couldn't understand why an otherwise charming little thing could become so spiteful in the presence of the priest who had tried to befriend her on many occasions.

Once when Don Mario, on his way back from attending a sick parishioner, arrived at the house of the vet bringing her some nuts as a kind of peace offering, the monkey attacked him so viciously that she caused some holy water he was carrying in a cruet to be spilled. A few drops fell on the monkey who shrank in terror and, with a horrifying yell, went berserk, tearing apart the flat before disappearing for ever through a hole in a corner of the kitchen leaving burn marks all around.

The poor vet, left alone in his nearly destroyed flat, never fully recovered from the shock of this ghastly experience and, after a heart attack, went about half paralysed.

"Inscrutable are the ways of the Lord," concluded the old nun with great satisfaction. "Who knows what He has in store for those of us who are lacking in faith?"

After such a devastating tale I was sent home to meditate on the many facets of the devil and to pray (once more) for enlightenment. In fact, I went home shaking with fright and that evening, sitting on my father's knee, I repeated to him the story that the old nun had told us. That caused an explosion on the part of my father. He was given to sudden bursts of anger which, in general, went away as quickly as they came, but this time he threatened to take me away from the convent forthwith. Mother eventually succeeded in calming him down and, for once, I was allowed to go to sleep with the light on after drinking a cup of camomile and honey.

Next day father marched off to have a talk with the Mother Superior. As a result of that conversation I was left mostly to myself for the remaining period of instruction which proceeded smoothly enough. But no amount of kneeling in front of the altar in prayer or the fear of the Devil himself were really any good. I remained unconvinced.

First Communion

Still, the day of the first communion finally arrived. An old photograph taken after the great event, shows a little girl looking angelic and demure. She is wearing a long white gown and a white veil is held on her head by a coronet of flowers. She has a lily in one hand and a rosary in the other.

To my mother's greatest relief I behaved beautifully during the whole ceremony.

Before being posted to Libya my father had to undertake some training and was sent to a military airport somewhere in Tuscany. Mother and I had joined him and we took a villa for about six months in a beautiful place between the sea and the hills of the hinterland which gently sloped down to the coast. Vineyards amid olive trees stretched all around us and, here and there, maybe at a bend of a road, a lonely cypress stood guard at a little chapel.

The eighteenth century villa belonged to some friends of my parents and was full of exquisite furniture of that period. It had an Italian garden and the long drive leading to it was lined with dark cypress trees and bushes of oleanders.

It was spring when we arrived and everything was in bloom. The pink roses climbing up the old walls of the house and the lemon trees in their terracotta pots, outside on the porch. Behind the villa the blue hills were splashed with the yellow of the broom bushes and of late blossoming mimosas.

I took to the place immediately and went about exploring each room and up to the attic where the owners kept the most interesting looking trunks and boxes.

"What will they be keeping in them?" I asked myself, ready to find out but all too soon I heard my mother's voice calling me and spoiling all the fun of the discovery. "Clementina, come down at once, do you hear, you are not to touch anything up there." Next I went down to the cellar which was full of bottles and huge spiders' webs.

Another pleasant thing was the fact that Aunt Elena had come to spend some time with us. Father and I were extremely fond of her but mother liked her a lot less, possibly because she considered her too eccentric, especially now that she was a widow and had, once again, filled up her house with all sorts of pets. And she had come with her box of special cigars whose pungent smell mother detested!

I can't quite remember Aunt Elena's eccentricities, perhaps because I was supposed to be so much like her that I understood and approved everything she did or said, but I remember clearly daddy coming home with a gander.

He actually walked in carrying the animal himself. As he had arrived straight from the office in the full-dress uniform of colonel squeezing the gander against the ribbons of medals pinned on his chest, he made quite an odd entrance. Mother and I were sitting in the drawing room having just finished our tea with Aunt Elena dreamingly puffing at one of her cigars, apparently blissfully unaware of mother's irritation at the smoke which went straight into her face.

Daddy came in directly to greet us and he put the gander on the floor. It was a young bird with white feathers and a yellow beak. It didn't seem especially frightened or surprised to find itself in a drawing room but looked around with interest, honking once or twice as if it also wished to greet us politely.

"Here we are," daddy said to me with a grin. "Look what I have brought for you!" He was immediately interrupted by my mother who was wearing her disapproving expression generally reserved for me. "What on earth are you doing with that animal?" she asked him. "Why didn't you give it to Paolo (daddy's batman) to carry it straight to the kitchen?" "Impossible," said my father, very much tongue in cheek, "First of all Paolo isn't allowed to carry animals when he is wearing his uniform and, secondly, I didn't bring Caesar Augustus home to be put in a pot."

"Caesar Augustus!" we all exclaimed in surprise, "Why call a gander Caesar Augustus?"

"Because," replied my father sitting down in an armchair and putting me on his knee, "Caesar Augustus is a very special gander."

Daddy had actually just come back from a parade in honour of a German air marshal who was visiting Italy on an official tour. He had landed at the military airport and daddy had had to go and meet him and then escort him around.

They had been watching an air display, and other manifestations presently culminating in a big parade in honour of the guest. They were all standing to attention as the military band began to play the German national anthem when my father was appalled to see a gander sneaking through the rows of people gathered to watch the show and starting to walk towards the big brass. He walked slowly and solemnly putting one crooked leg in front of the other. The V.I.P.s looked at each other in embarrassment but remained immobile. The gander kept advancing towards them and, when he was a few inches away from the German officer, he looked up at him and, as father described it, delicately laid some droppings at his feet!

"Do you see why I had to rescue him?" continued my father

with an air of satisfaction. "I really couldn't let him be punished or maybe made into a mascot . . . As it is, by the time I left, the story had made the round of the airport and everybody was immensely amused. Except for the Germans of course!"

Sitting on daddy's knee and listening to his extraordinary story, I could see that mother had some difficulty in believing him; moreover she wasn't interested in animals and could never understand why daddy and I were so fond of them.

Aunt Elena, on the contrary, seemed very amused and interested. She had a great love for animals and whenever she came to stay with us she took along with her photographs of all her pets which she would put on display on the chest of drawers in her bedroom, and daddy would advise me to ask after them before enquiring about anything else!

"What a splendid gander," she now exclaimed enthusiastically. "Of course he must be looked after and kept here with us." And in fact the gander was allowed to stay and went to live in the courtyard together with the poultry.

I also remember very well my last day at the villa. It was grape harvest time. The bells of the little churches had been pealing merrily since the early morning and the hills were swarming with people who had come to help with the *vendemmia*. Big bunches of luscious grapes, turgid with juice, were ready to be plucked. All day I busied myself helping the women in the orchard and helping myself to a great quantity of sticky green and purple figs which they had picked to fill large wicker baskets. They were delicious, some so ripe that they had split open revealing their inviting red pulp, so inviting that, towards the end of the day, I had to go indoors to nurse a terrific and well-deserved tummy-ache.

All night I toiled keeping my poor mother up. Next day we were to sail to Tripoli and when the car which was going to take us to Genoa harbour arrived, I was feeling distinctly sorry for myself!

Chapter Four

LIBYA 1937–39

In the early autumn of 1937 we arrived at Tripoli, "the end of the world" as far as my mother was concerned!

The voyage by boat from Genoa to Tripoli was full of delight for me but my mama was seasick most of the time and had to lie down on her berth whilst daddy and I braved the waves and remained on deck.

Life on board was fun. I adored the sea and would watch it for hours taking in all its changeable moods and shades of colour. I explored the ship, up on the bridge and down in the engine-room and, being away from my mother's strict control, I felt free to roam about and stuff myself with all the delicious food one could have at the captain's table. No more insipid stuff which was supposed to be good for me. No more "Eat your food, Clementina, at once!" or her pleading with me "One spoonful for mama, one for daddy . . ." Now I ate everything put in front of me with great relish and I ate it up quickly and with my best table manners because I felt very grown-up sitting there in mother's place across the table from daddy.

He was the best companion I could have, having become a kind of superman in my young eyes, someone who could be so kind and amusing and knowledgeable and go to war and come back with some splendid shining medals and now he was going to fly a plane! Although his life style had so dramatically changed in the last few years, he had maintained a sense of humour about himself and instead of wallowing in self-pity for allowing himself to be so badly cheated by a so-called friend, he had preferred to blame the world depression for all his financial problems. Nevertheless it must have been very hard for him to adapt to his new life, unused as he had been to make ends meet. Later in his life, when things got worse, he was to suffer abominably for lack of money but now he gave me the impression that it was all part of a game and that the important thing was to play the game well. I adored him for that and was immensely proud of him and of the fact that people said that I looked exactly like him!

Libya was then a colony of Italy. Its governor, Air Force Marshal Italo Balbo, had been one of the *Quadrumviri* the men who led with Mussolini the famous *Marcia su Roma* (March on Rome) back in 1922, when the Fascists took over the government of Italy. He was a dashing, out-spoken man and it was rumoured that he had been banished to the colonies, away from the corridors of power in Rome, because of his opposition to Mussolini's policy of friendship with Germany. He was to be killed in 1940 at the beginning of the war, near Tobruk when the airplane he was flying crashed after being hit by Italian anti-aircraft fire during a British bombardment. At the time of our arrival, he was full of enthusiasm and hope of making part of the Sahara Desert fertile again as it was during the time of the Roman Empire. He took a great liking to my father who had to spend a lot of time in his company.

Colonial life surprisingly agreed with my parents and I think the fact that my father was able to earn some money without the danger of being killed in a war had a lot to do with it. I loved the warmth of the climate, the nearness to the sea, the Arabs with the pungent smell of their souks, and what I had seen of the desert. It was fun living there; most of the year the weather was warm enough to go to the beach and swim and I was often taken outside the town to an oasis for a picnic. Then there were the excursions on the fringe of the desert. The Bedouin living there in their tents would give us food which we would eat with our hands sitting on rugs on the floor. Sometimes they would offer my father a sheep or a goat which one couldn't refuse without offending them. I remember that once they even insisted on putting the poor animal in the boot of our car!

I was of course immediately sent off to school, which mercifully was only in the morning. Back in Milan my first two years of elementary school had been pleasant enough as I was taught, together with the children of my parents' friends, by some undemanding nuns. Here the class was much more mixed and we had a teacher, Miss Bianchi, who was a middle-aged spinster and what was then called a practising Fascist. She lived and worked in the spirit of the Fascist ideology and was a keen member of the party. When she entered the class-room, we had to greet her standing up and lifting our right arm in the Fascist salute shouting "Viva il Duce". It was called then the Roman salute because that was the way our glorious ancestors greeted each other. Then she would inspect each one of us in turn, slowly walking around the desks while we continued to stand to attention. Usually we wore white cotton overalls, the girls had a pink bow tied at the collar, the boys a pale blue one. But on special occasions we had to wear the Fascist uniform of *i figli della Lupa* (the children of the she-wolf). This strange name recalled the origin of Rome, whose founders, Romulus and Remus, were allegedly suckled by a she-wolf. Out of school we had to join innumerable parades, marching and singing patriotic songs. But, in the class-room when, after Miss Bianchi's inspection, we sang the national anthem, I was invariably excused from singing it because I was so out of tune that my thin voice could be noticed even among thirty others!

After this, Miss Bianchi would stop in front of a picture of Mussolini which hung on the wall and lifting once more her right arm in the Fascist salute, she would dedicate her day (and ours) to him, promising in a loud voice to instruct us in his precepts.

We were expected to talk to her using the form *voi* instead of the usual *lei* to which I was accustomed. This new way of addressing people was another of Mussolini's ideas but I can't quite remember the reason for it. Anyway, I started off with Miss Bianchi on the wrong foot by not using it in addressing her, as I had never heard of it before. "Don't you ever speak like that to me again," she said to me sharply, "Where do you come from?" I hardly dared to tell her that the nuns never, but never, saluted in such a way nor did they use that new form of address!

But I soon got used to my new surroundings and settled down quite happily. I was nine-years-old, already quite disobedient but certainly not fussy about my teachers' little fixations: if one wanted us to say a prayer in front of the crucifix and the next one smartly to salute Mussolini's pictures it was all right by me. I was quite uninterested in either of them for the time being. All I really cared about was to go and play on the sea-shore. How I loved that!

During the cold months when I wasn't allowed to go to the beach my great passion was still reading. Lying flat on my tummy

on the white thick carpet of my bedroom, I would spend my
afternoons enthralled by the extraordinary adventures of Jules
Verne and Emilio Salgari, saddened by De Amici's *Cuore* or
thrilled by Pinocchio and other children's heroes. All these books
were chosen for me with great care by my parents or by my
teacher. The school had a large library and there, among the
classics, one could find little booklets which Miss Bianchi strongly
advised her pupils to borrow. They contained instructive stories in
which good little Fascist girls, by doing things in the good Fascist
way, were invariably handsomely rewarded. The good Fascist way
of educating children required a high standard of morality; great
stress was put on the virtues of honesty, fairness and cleanliness,
and one was encouraged to love one's country, to work hard, to
respect and obey one's parents and one's teachers. I suppose, very
much on the lines of 'king and country'.

But, unlike English children, we were encouraged to imitate the
way of life of the glorious Romans, as that part of Italian history
was very popular with the Fascist regime. And, of course, we were
made to believe that all those shining virtues were typical Fascist
virtues.

I was very impressionable and the adventure books would excite
me out of the ordinary and make me dream and wonder. I would
identify myself with the part of the heroine and pretend to be like
her. I remember that once, having read a story about a little girl
who had lost her voice, I wouldn't speak for a whole day and, to
my mother's great irritation, I refused to answer her questions.

In such cases I was again reprimanded for using my imagination.
"Pretending to be what one is not is a form of lying," I was told.
"Remember what happened to Pinocchio." But I didn't care.
Being an only child I was often alone by myself and I couldn't bear
to be bored. So I retreated to my world of make-believe where
everything was exciting and larger than life. Besides, I had heard a
friend of my father's saying that "Imagination was a gift of the
gods". Why was it that the grown-ups never agreed on anything? I
was very anti grown-ups during that time because I had just
realised that Father Christmas didn't exist and that the stork didn't
bring the new babies after all. I had appealed for enlightenment to
my parents and they had to admit that Father Christmas didn't
come down the chimney (there wasn't one in our house in Tripoli)

but they made feeble excuses for not giving me a truthful answer about babies. I asked myself, full of indignation, who had been lying? I remember my sense of disappointment in realising that even daddy hadn't been completely fair with me and from then on my complete faith in the word of the grown-ups was badly shaken.

The source of this imprecise information about the non-existence of Father Christmas and the doubtful birth of babies came from my new bosom friend, Donatella. She was short and plump with long raven hair and a magnolia skin which I greatly envied. She was the same age as myself and we were in the same class-room where she sat just behind me. She had two older brothers and she knew all sorts of things for which she had all my admiration, though she couldn't quite tell me how babies came about. She knew how boys were made and why parents slept together (because they promised the priest to do so when they got married) and she knew how to make a cake and how to knit a scarf.

Donatella's people came from Sardinia. They had different customs and, to a certain extent, a different outlook on life than my parents who came from the North of Italy. Still, I suppose, one had to fraternise in the colonies and so they saw a lot of one another. We would generally meet them on Sundays after Mass at the church door and walk a short distance to a coffee bar.

I don't remember much of Tripoli's topography, but its High Street is clearly defined in my mind with its porticoes and the Arab bazaars at the far end of the street. This is because every Sunday morning, as I have just mentioned, my parents and I would go there to a coffee bar to buy little cakes and tarts which we would take home for our Sunday luncheon. It was customary then as it is still today in Italy that, after having paid one's respect to God, so to speak, and after having listened to one hour long High Mass and a sermon, one would indulge oneself in such innocent small pleasures of the flesh. The grown-ups would have an aperitif and discuss the latest gossip, and we children would be allowed one small cake or two. I was inordinately fond of little marzipan cakes which stood in a line under a glass counter. They were made in the shape of an upright frog, filled with green cream. At times I had to endure what I believed to be the most unfair form of reprisal from my mother. If she thought that I hadn't behaved properly in church, such as turning my head around or, worse still, chatting with a neighbour, she would forbid me to eat the cakes. I would be standing there near the counter gaping at Donatella and the other children contentedly munching away, tears slowly rolling down my cheeks, indeed looking not unlike the little donkey we had recently discovered.

One day Donatella and I were slowly walking down a path between palm groves on our way back from school and carrying our satchels with straps on our shoulders. We were discussing a boy in our class whom we thought particularly stupid (in our eyes, boys were uninteresting little chaps who wanted to play football all the time. We also thought they smelled). We heard a sound of braying at the nearby hut.

"Listen, a donkey," cried Donatella, all thoughts of silly boys quickly disappearing from her before the excitement of playing with a donkey, "Let's go and see." A little donkey was shading himself from the sun under a tree. He was small and had enormous dark velvet eyes and long eyelashes. The flies which settled in the corners of his eyes made them water, as if he were softly crying, giving him an air of gentle melancholy. His owner, a poor trader, was lying down on a mat next to him. Obviously, like many other Arabs, he must have been riding him without a saddle, keeping his balance by lazily swinging his legs on the side, and spurring him on by poking his neck with a sharp pointed piece of wood. This had eventually caused the sore we could see on the animal's neck, a raw and bloody patch, black with flies.

"Let's do something for him, let's take him home!" Donatella exclaimed. Her house had a nice garden and there was certainly room for a donkey there. We had started stroking and patting him until the Arab, furious at being disturbed in his sleep, got up and told us to go away and threw pebbles at us. We ran all the way to Donatella's place but unfortunately her parents were not at all interested in the little donkey's plight and wouldn't even consider the possibility of having him in their garden. And so, for the time being, we had to content ourselves with visiting him now and then, taking with us some carrots and carobs.

I often went to play at Donatella's house, sometimes spending the night with her and was often escorted there by daddy's batman, Paolo who, we thought, was soft on her cook, Margherita.

The Donkey

Margherita was a big, strong woman, dark-skinned with flashing black eyes and even blacker hair and a shade of a moustache on her upper lip. She was quick to laugh, showing a beautiful set of white teeth. She had "bumps in all the right places", as Paolo was fond of describing her. But she also had a foul temper and a dark past; she had in fact killed a man. It had all happened some years before, back in Sardinia. She was then a young girl living in a village at the foot of some rugged hills where only shepherds walked with their dogs and grazing sheep, and bandits hid in caves. She had been promised in marriage to a young man, a farrier, who lived in the next village. They were going to be married in the summer. That spring Margherita spent long hours sitting on a chair outside the door of her house preparing her modest dowry, sewing and embroidering sheets and towels and pretty petticoats. She watched her young man passing by in his cart or, perhaps, leading a mule back to his owner, waving at her. "How handsome and strong he is!" she must have thought looking at him. "A real man!" Then, as spring gave away to summer and the days became

longer and warmer, he stopped coming her way. She became
suspicious and started spying on him. One evening at dusk she saw
him walking fast towards the hills. She picked up her brother's gun
and followed him. A girl was waiting for him near a bush and
together they began walking slowly towards the caves. Margherita
called out to him. He turned around and a bullet went through his
chest killing him on the spot.

This was the official story and Margherita was arrested and
taken to trial. She pleaded innocent according to Sardinia's code
of honour of that time: she had killed to defend her honour. The
judge set her free.

She left the village and went to Cagliari to seek work. The
Sardinians understood all about crimes of honour and soon
Margherita found an honourable position with Donatella's family.
She was a magnificent cook.

Both Paolo and I were fascinated by her story, but being far less
understanding than her employers, when she set her dark eyes on
him, he couldn't help a shudder of fear! However, nothing
dramatically happened in his case and often they sat in the kitchen
over a glass of wine while we girls had a little snack.

It must have been a few months after we had discovered our little
donkey that Miss Pringle arrived. She was English and my father's
old nanny. She had continued to stay with the family long after
daddy had gone away to school but for many years now she had
lived in a small hotel with a companion, somewhere on Lake
Como. She adored daddy and had kept in touch with him all these
years and now she had come to visit us. She looked ancient to me
and walked with a stick. Her Italian was most peculiar and her
accent extremely funny, although she had spent over forty years in
Italy. She told me that I reminded her of my father when he was
my age and that she had noticed that I had inherited the same bad
habit of picking my nose. In fact, she told me to stop picking my
nose dozens of times and Donatella and I called her Miss Pick
Nose behind her back. But we had to admit that she was also truly
marvellous because when she agreed to come with us to inspect
our little donkey she declared that the way he had been treated
was disgraceful and she promised she would do something about
it.

She hit on the idea of hiring him out for children's garden parties. My mother was asked to get in touch with other ladies to see whether they could be interested in her plan and the trader was summoned to our house. He soon broke out in smiles when he heard what we had in mind for him and a deal was quickly made. He would provide the donkey with a small saddle so that the children could ride him around their gardens, and if he looked after the donkey properly he would be paid a generous retainer. The trader quickly agreed to all this and Donatella and I were ecstatic.

A week later Donatella's birthday came up and her parents hired the little donkey for their garden party. He arrived in full regalia, a clean white cloth under his new saddle and a flower fixed in his headgear. He announced his arrival by braying, trotting briskly through the open gates, and was greeted by the shouts of us children. He was an immense success and soon other people hired him. In fact, only the war broke up this happy arrangement and the little donkey and Miss Pringle, much like the rest of us, were engulfed in the horrors that followed.

These are some of the people that I best remember of my days in Tripoli but then there were others like Ali and Mohamed, the two batmen who replaced Paolo when for some reason which I can't quite remember, he had to go back to Italy.

While Mohamed was an easy-going type, always cheerful and smiling, Ali, a small, dark-skinned Arab was highly-strung and, it seemed to me, often in a tense mood. Apparently this was due to the fact that we had engaged a Jewish girl by the name of Fortuna as a cook, and he couldn't accept the presence of a Jewess in the household. In fact one day he asked to see my father for personal reasons. Audience granted, he stood to attention and asked permission to throw Fortuna out of the house. "Permission not granted," said my father. "Then, sir," Ali replied very seriously, "I shall set fire to her pigtails." Actually he never went so far but he frightened her so much with his animosity that she had to leave us to be replaced by an Italian girl.

Ali was also very loyal and simple-minded and once, when my father fell ill and mother and I were away, he looked after him day and night and never left his bedside, sleeping on the floor outside the bedroom door. In answer to father's request to go away and get some proper sleep he replied that he wanted to be present when my father died!

My Father

But daddy had other problems. In those last years before the war, Mussolini seemed to have succeeded in impressing Hitler with the efficiency of the Italian armed forces in the colonies. I remember my father coming home from escorting various foreign guests, red in the face with rage and indignation at the tomfoolery of these exhibitions of Italian might. High-ranking German officers came to visit Libya—Marshal Goering was among them—and later some Japanese. For each visit a great display was laid on with parades, army exercises, aerobatics. These shows were designed to give our dear *camerati* the impression that we had much more military strength stationed in Libya than was the case and often the same planes flew in formation again and again over the parade ground.

When we had first arrived in Tripoli we lived for a short time in midtown but later we moved to a house overlooking the sea. Next to it was the villa of a general whose wife was a member of the Italian royal family. My parents saw a lot of them and I played now and then with their daughters. Meeting them led to an interesting development, as later on, when we had to return to Italy during the first year of the war, my mother and I were asked to stay with them.

Although I was a lot happier in Tripoli than in Milan, my relationship with mother didn't improve. Perhaps I was a difficult child because I remember being scolded and punished a lot by her. But mother had a way of twisting things round when complaining about me to my father or to her friends which, I felt, was terribly unfair. It would make me literally choke with fury and I couldn't utter a single word in my defence. On the contrary, I would idiotically burst into tears. And she was over-protective, discouraging me from playing with other children and making me think that I was delicate and always in need of rest. So, by reaction, I came to believe that children should be told instead to grasp life with both hands, be daring and optimistic. "It's better to catch a cold, wet feet and all," I told her years later, "than to grow up being timid and insecure. Children should be encouraged to do things, not to be restrained by endless don'ts." But, be that as it may, my mother never subscribed to this philosophy of mine and there I was, always in trouble for trying to disobey her!

"Clementina, don't slouch about, don't point, don't interrupt when I'm talking, don't bite your nails . . ." So many other embarrassing remarks about my looks, my voice, my clumsiness, often ending with the phrase: "You will regret it when you are forty." But forty was so far away and so *old* that it wasn't possible to imagine. Other times, looking sadly at me and shaking her head, she would say: 'How different you are from me, no one would have thought that you are a daughter of mine." And just as well, I would think on such occasions, I didn't want to be like her at all. Not at all, in spite of the fact that she was very well preserved and very smart and would often receive with a grateful enchanting smile the praise of the people who admired her.

I didn't know what I wanted to be but emphatically not what my mother represented to me. She seemed to lead such a boring existence, always following the same old routine and going to parties because it was her duty to do so and not because they were fun. There was always a great deal of talk about duty and her life seemed very monotonous without the pleasures and the games I played.

I suppose that the grown-ups, because of the seriousness of the world situation, were mostly in a concerned and depressed frame of mind, often complaining about life being difficult and the necessity of being patient: "You will find out when you grow up," they would say with a sigh and with what seemed almost perverse satisfaction if we children asked the reason for their pessimism; how boring all that was and how discouraging!

Mother was a very tidy and precise person and had a horror of waste: she couldn't bear to waste time or anything else. No left-overs were ever thrown away and clothes were worn to the bitter thread as my father jokingly used to say. Often she would send his civilian suits, which had been made by a very good tailor, to a convent nearby where the patient novices would unpick them and then sew them up again inside out, making them look like new. But because she was very refined and fussy, on the whole, she bought good quality clothes from the best shops. She believed that it was far better to have fewer but well-made dresses than a lot of rubbish. She always bought classic garments as she had strict ideas about what a lady should wear. Years later, she would reproach me for buying cheap things which "every middle-class girl would be wearing", disregarding my need for more variety and my lack of money.

In spite of her generosity from which no one was really ever excluded, she kept a tight budget, frowning on any hint of extravagance that daddy and I might have suggested. Sometimes daddy would sharply react to these restrictions and then they would quarrel and how boring that was also!

Going to the beach was one of the few things I was always

allowed to do because mother believed that the sea air was beneficial to one's health, as was the pure transparent sea water which contained iodine and was not to be showered away from one's body after a swim! How well I remember my happiness in waking up in the morning knowing that the first thing I would do was to go down to the beach. I liked the sea so much; I liked the big waves and I didn't mind being tossed and turned upside down with the foam getting in my eyes and nose, I liked watching my long hair float in the water, the salt on my skin, the sense of sheer exhaustion after a long swim, I liked to lie on the beach near the sea where the sand was wet and the waves came up and washed all over you, and I liked to collect every type of shell that I could find, and store them away carefully in a drawer near my bed. These memories of almost sensual pleasure are the ones which stick out more vividly in my mind when I try to recall my years in Tripoli; the rest seems to have been covered and swept away by the sands of the desert.

In 1939 we went to Italy on home leave. This was going to be my father's last holiday. As it was, with talk of war everywhere, he wasn't much in the frame of mind to enjoy it. Ideologically Fascism didn't appeal to him and having had in his work a taste of the Nazi arrogance and ruthlessness he could only view the turn of events with great concern. He might also have thought that having fought in two wars was just about enough for any man.

On our way to the north of Italy, we stopped for a day in Rome. I had never been there before and it made an unforgettable impression on me. I had been studying that very year about the old Romans and I was delighted to be able actually to stroll on the Forum which was now a large garden with oleanders growing all along the Via Sacra, and walk up to the Palatine. Amazing! It was due to Mussolini that this ancient part of Rome was now so well looked after but his presence was also felt in modern Rome whose walls were literally covered with his slogans like *Credere-Obbedire-Combattere* (Believe-Obey-Fight) or the dashing *E' meglio vivere un giorno da leone che cento da pecora* (It's better to live a day like a lion than a hundred like a sheep) and many others which I knew all by heart. And the capital was swarming with Black Shirts. I noticed that many people gave them the right of way along the pavement. Father was outraged, no one gave him the right of way even if he was wearing his uniform when he had to call at the Air Ministry!

It was in Rome that I heard for the first time—*viva voce*—Mussolini making a speech. Quite naturally being so young and having been born into it, I took Fascism for granted and didn't question it. My father's grumblings were to a great extent part of the grown-up world and, in general, my mother discouraged him from talking politics in front of me, afraid that I would repeat what I heard and put his job in jeopardy.

All the same, standing uncomfortably in a square packed with sweaty, shouting humanity, I found myself looking at the Duce with great curiosity and excitement. I could see him very clearly from where I stood but I found him much older than I expected, too fat, entirely bald and slightly vulgar. He moved his hands about a great deal and when he put them on his hips, sticking his chin out at the same time, in the now so well-known posture, he seemed prepared to play ball with the world with the same confidence and in the same way he had played so far successfully with Italy. The people about me were applauding him madly and enthusiastically. His speech went on and on and soon I felt like fainting. I looked up at my father for help but he looked cross and red in the face. At the same time my mother looked at us both and was quite alarmed by my pallor and his crimson colour. Very wisely, before I could pass out and daddy could have a fit (*Un colpo apopletico* as she would call it), she started to push a way out of the crowd murmuring something about her poor child and with great difficulty we managed to get out. This experience entirely ruined our day in the Eternal City. My father was quite convinced that we would go to war and had an argument with mother who firmly believed that the king would keep us out of it. (Later when the war had indeed been declared she was under the misconception that *gli Inglesi* would never bomb and destroy our beautiful historic cities but unfortunately and all too soon the English proved her wrong!)

After a few days in the Dolomites all leave was cancelled and daddy went back to Tripoli ahead of us. We joined him later but the rest of my stay in Libya was a time of gloom, quarrels and general uneasiness among the grown-ups which affected also us children.

The Allies were at war with Germany, of course, and everybody was wondering what Italy would do. Well, on 10th June, 1940, Italy declared war on England and France.

Mother and I went on board the last passenger ship going to Italy leaving behind my father and my beloved shell collection!

Chapter Five

THE WAR YEARS

As I have already mentioned, during our stay in Tripoli my parents had become well acquainted with some members of the Italian royal family who were also stationed in the colony. When mother and I had to leave Libya because of the imminence of the war, they asked us to join them for the summer months at the royal residence of San Rossore.

San Rossore was a vast beautiful estate with forests of stone pine which bordered the sea, patches of maremma land where dromedaries lazily browsed in the sunshine, woods full of deer, ponies and wild boars. The river which crossed it had lots of fish and, as I firmly believed then, nymphs who hid from us children during the day only to come out at night to sing for Pan, the rural god. Its beaches were white with beautiful clean sand which hid the many-coloured shells and the sea, like everything else there, held a magic of its own.

The people living in this estate went about their way on horse-drawn carriages and up in the large house, surrounded by their court, there lived a king and a queen.

San Rossore was indeed an enchanting place by any standard, but to me in particular, it was simply wonderland!

Mother and I had arrived one day in mid-June having gone straight there after landing at Genoa harbour two days after the beginning of the war.

My mother had insisted on making me rehearse the curtsy I was going to make when presented to the members of the royal family practically from the moment she had received the invitation. On board the ship which took us sadly away from daddy and Africa I was given instructions on how to behave in front of them. The continuous rolling of the boat turned those instructions into a comic affair because mother insisted on showing me how deeply I had to bow between her bouts of seasickness and with me falling, more often than not, flat on my bottom.

The day after our arrival there we were presented to the king and queen and, although the atmosphere of San Rossore was very informal, there was a great number of people to whom one had to curtsy. Mother made her round dutifully followed by me, but bewildered as she was, she made one of her beautiful deep curtsies also to a governess!

I was really frightened at meeting the king, who looked aloof and distant, but the queen with her reassuringly warm smile made me feel at ease immediately. She taught me later how to knit and, as part of the war effort, I was soon to make sweaters and socks for the sailors. The wool was coarse and prickly and it strongly smelled of sheep. Poor sailors, some of those socks I knitted could easily have fitted the foot of an elephant!

There were quite a lot of children that summer at San Rossore and we were merry and joyful and played all day long to our hearts' content, blissfully unaware of the war raging in the outside world.

In the morning we would go to the seaside in horse-drawn carriages and stay there until noon. Lunch was a very gay, informal affair with simple but delicious food served by man-servants. We would sit at the table with the grown-ups and were allowed to talk. I remember that we were often given *crème caramel* as dessert and that, every time this was served, one of us would whisper the word "eels" in an attempt at putting the others off their pudding which, no matter what, had to be finished. And this because we had seen that the yellow stuff eels spit out, when caught, bears a disturbing resemblance to *crème caramel*. Also—bad-mannered brats that we were—we would sometimes use out middle finger to shovel food on to a fork, or more than accidentally, spill water or wine on the table-cloth . . . mother couldn't believe her eyes!

After lunch we were sent to rest for a while. I remember a boy called Gianni spending his resting time playing with huge black ants near the French window of my bedroom. I would spy on him, fascinated, through the opening of the shutters, watching him mark his territory with white chalk, five, six feet each way, and wait. Any ant that would cross his border would be picked up and carefully inspected. Then he would take out his penknife and proceed very slowly to cut off its legs, one by one, and finally, its head. Small red ants were allowed to walk through. Once he saw me watching him and, in a fit of fury, he quickly got up and stabbed my two fingers which were keeping the shutters ajar. "Don't tell," he said to me menacingly, "Or I'll do to you what I do to my ants!" I didn't breathe a word but it took me quite a bit to convince mother that I had cut my fingers peeling an apple. "I always say that you have horrid table manners," she commented drily.

In the afternoon and early evening we went walking or cycling in the woods; sometimes we played ping-pong or tennis and went fishing. When fishing from a boat in the river we used a rod with a cord attached. One end of the cord was connected to the rod and the other end had a heavy piece of lead tied to it. Worms were tied to the lead by string. The cord was long enough to touch the bottom of the river. By bouncing the lead on the river-bed we attracted the attention of the eels who came and ate the worms. The string became caught between their teeth and we would feel a pull on the cord. We became very skilled in this method taught us by local fishermen and very seldom lost an eel. But, all the same, we didn't like to be reminded of it at the dining-table!

At other times we would fish at the mouth of the river with normal fishing tackle, together with the fishermen and their nets.

We had dinner by ourselves: a riotous affair in which those young members of the royal family and their cousins tried to be as mischievous as their strict governess allowed. After it, the time left before bed was spent playing games or watching films. Twice, they must have been special occasions, a magician came to entertain us. Before my very eyes I saw rabbits coming out of top hats, scarves changing colours, people being hypnotised and made to believe that they were on a bicycle, riding furiously across a chair. Mother was made to feel very hot and she started taking off her clothes! I was spellbound!

All too soon the summer came to an end and gradually the leaves began to change colour and the woods looked even more beautiful with great patches of cyclamens scattered under its trees. The thought of school was brought to our minds by the adults' repeated exhortations to take out our books. We were not a very studious lot and in Tripoli we didn't work too hard, but now we had to face a school year in Italy. We were all going to Rome to live in a villa surrounded by acres of woodland. And so we did.

Nothing very much seems to have happened to us children during that school year in Rome. We would go to school in the morning by horse and trap to the state school nearby (not even the king's grandchildren went to a private school), do our homework in the afternoon and play among ourselves in the grounds. We seldom left the property, but sometimes other children came to play with us. That winter it snowed in Rome and we went sledging. In the spring most of the young people went down with measles, one after the other, until only a young German prince and I were left to run around. We kept each other company walking around the park hand in hand and picking wild asparagus which would be cooked for us later for dinner. How well I remember him, a shy, dreamy boy who could paint so well, who was so kind and friendly and the first boy who made me blush and feel embarrassed.

Once I was taken to the opera house with some of the king's grandchildren. What fun it was being applauded and acclaimed with them whilst the whole audience stood up and cheered us.

In the spring of 1941 we had not yet felt the full brunt of the war and there were still some people who thought we could win it. We children at the palace, safely protected by the walls surrounding the huge property, hardly gave a thought to it—or at least I didn't—and went about our way blissfully unsuspecting the great tragedy which was soon to engulf us all.

But suddenly summer was with us again and it brought to an end that extraordinary year in which I shared daily in the lives of royalty.

During that year my father had been in Libya all along "fighting for his king and country in the torrid depths of Africa" as mother was so fond of saying, but at just about the time we left Rome, he was struck by beri-beri, hospitalised, and eventually sent back to Italy. Beri-beri is a nutritional deficiency disease which is due primarily to a lack of adequate vitamin B1 in the diet, in which paralysis and waisting of muscles may occur. Father was struck in his legs and, for a while, he couldn't walk.

This marked the beginning of a long, unbelievably painful period for my parents and myself but, also, of course, for the Italian people in general. The *guerra lampo* (the quick war) was turning out to be a long agonising process.

We moved back to Milan where father could receive adequate medical attention and, when his health improved, he resumed his position as colonel, this time stationed at the air force base of Milan. He was a bit wobbly on his legs but with the help of a stick he could manage fairly well. What was slowly becoming apparent to me was his internal turmoil, the bitter dissatisfaction and the strong disapproval he felt about this war. When beri-beri struck him again some time later, this time paralysing his arms, he was relieved, almost glad, because this handicap enabled him to leave the service in an honourable way. Later we all realised that it had also saved him from being deported to Germany like so many of his fellow officers.

Father had a very quick temper; he could lose it in a flash, without giving us any warning. He would suddenly go all red in the face and explode at the slightest provocation generally about some trivia. This contrasted strongly with an other side of his nature; he would keep a perfect control over his temper when faced with something really serious. I used to be quite frightened of these outbursts of fury, especially when I was small. Soon, however, I realised that I had inherited this trait from him and, more often than not, I would react with equal exasperation to mother who, I thought, was a great source of provocation.

He continued to take a keen interest in my work at school and I was more than ever proud of him. I was immensely impressed by the way he had accepted his disabling illness and the more life became difficult for him the more I admired him. When he was in a good mood he could still be very funny and say the wittiest things and I was most grateful to him for opening my mind to beauty and culture. He would discuss poetry, literature and the theatre and talk about the great events of the past, giving me a much needed perspective about the history of the world which, not surprisingly, was taught in my school in the most sectarian way. For example, if in my book it was written that Italy had been united by Cavour and Garibaldi, he would stress the importance that Napoleon III had had in helping them to achieve their goal. Equally he would keep a balanced mind when expressing an opinion about the then often belittled *Perfidious-Albion,* of which he was a great admirer.

He was still my superman and I never doubted his judgement and deep knowledge. In fact, I thought him the most intelligent of men and none of my teachers was ever up to his level. He was often on my side during important discussions with mother, but whenever he thought that the issue was unimportant for my education, he would not interfere in our petty squabbles, often curtly enjoining me to do "what mummy tells you". In such cases I would become more stubborn than ever as, I suspect, I was jealous of her intimacy with him; no doubt I was getting into what she called the difficult age.

However, little by little, daddy's unhappiness about the war and his debilitating disease made him lose one of his greatest gifts, his zest for life; he became rather sad and quiet with only brief and much less frequent outbursts of temper. And I almost missed those lively blow-ups.

At the same time, but how much more devastatingly, all over Italy houses and people were blown up as the Allied bombing of the Italian cities began in earnest. The street lamps went out at night and the windows of the houses were covered with thick dark paper so that no light could be seen from the outside. Often the sirens would start wailing in the middle of the night and I would hear people running to the nearest shelter. Mother, disappointed as she was by the incredible lack of chivalry of the English, would come to my room and make me go down with her and the other tenants to the cellar where we would wait, cold and sleepy, for the all clear. I was then a rather unsettled and insecure teenager but, strangely enough, I took the bombing in my stride. Perhaps I was just irresponsible, *incosciente* as my mother would say, not conscious of the reality of danger and I rather enjoyed all the upheaval and the disorder in our lives.

Soon people were leaving the big cities in large numbers; new worlds like *evacuare* and *sfollati* (war evacuees) began to become familiar. We too, like so many other people, tried to look for a new home in the country. But the price of any type of accommodation outside town had immediately gone up so that for the time being, at least, we decided to stay in Milan a while longer.

I had been sent to a new school which was not far from where we were living. I was rather an erratic student but had an extraordinarily good memory, and I could memorise everything without really going deeply into it. Having chosen a classical education I went through eight years of Latin and five of Greek. One could find literal translations available for all the passages we had to translate from either language and I dutifully memorised the lot, by simply reading them once or twice in the evening before going to bed and once again in the morning before lessons. My teacher could stop me in the middle of my recital, ask me a question or two, get me started on another page and I would sail through without hesitation. I generally got top marks in all classical subjects. My weak spot was maths and sadly the only teacher who ever managed to hold my interest in it for a time was killed during a bombardment, just when I was beginning to understand the basics of fractions.

But I could be an eager student if a subject interested me and I would then plunge into it with all the power of concentration at my disposal and quickly master it. Generally, though, I found the mechanics of studying very boring and I had difficulties in applying myself with the needed discipline to my task. Details and dates infuriated me and I was easily discouraged by any subject which required patience and precision.

School in those years of the Fascist regime, also meant endless hours spent in expressing and practising the various rites of its ideology. There were the immense gatherings of the people (*le adunate oceaniche*), the assemblies, the musters in which school-children were obliged to appear in the Fascist uniform. Those rites were founded on a discipline of a militaristic type which forced men and women and especially young people, to wear some kind of uniform and turn up at different types of parades. There were the Fascist Saturdays, the campings in which one had to get up before dawn and perform arduous tasks, the more arduous the better; the physical training; the drills which ended as grotesque when some members of the Fascist hierarchy, obviously out of shape and sporting a considerable paunch, had to jump through a ring of fire!

Discipline in the schools was very strict and we were supposed to show our Fascist zeal in various ways from promptly leaping to attention in the Fascist salute, to reciting by heart the many slogans which our Duce coined from time to time. If taken seriously, being part of the Fascist Youth was a full-time occupation but for different reasons both my parents tried to keep me out of it; father, because he detested the Fascist ideology in all its forms and substance and was incapable of understanding people who took themselves so seriously and were so completely devoid of a sense of humour and went out of their way to make themselves look ridiculous. "Never heard of anybody so insensitive to the ridiculous," he used to say. Mother, on the other hand, thought that I was too fragile to stand up to the rigour of the various activities and she tried to shelter me from them by sending endless doctor's certificates proving my poor health, as often as the summons to one of those meetings came in the form of a card which was then collected at the gathering as proof of one's presence there.

Obviously with the coming of the war, these various manifestations were cut back as, a little later, all written examinations would be abolished.

So schooling and the frequent changes of teachers was not a problem and the daily routine was often enlivened by the scramble to the nearest shelter at whatever school I happened to be.

In spite of my irresponsibility, the last bombing of Milan before we eventually decided we had to move out to the countryside, made a lasting impression on me. Bombs had started dropping out of the sky more and more frequently, and one night, my school and the house next door to ours were hit and almost completely destroyed. My class-room, when I saw it the following morning, was just a heap of rubble, with no trace of desks or blackboard. On the remaining half of the only wall still left standing, the picture of our king still hung, crooked on its nail, the glass completely shattered out of the frame. They had come early the previous night, in a beautiful cloudless sky. My father and I were just coming back from a late stroll to our house which stood out in the square, tall and lit by the moonlight. Suddenly, a split second before the sirens shrieked their warning, we heard the fall of the first bombs. It took us completely by surprise and as we hastened to the shelter, daddy stumbled and almost fell on his wobbly legs. He was holding my hand and, unwittingly, he transmitted to me his fear and concern for my safety. For a moment I felt panic-stricken. The noise all around us was shattering; the raid was obviously aiming at the centre of the town, at its elegant old streets, at *La Scala,* at the *Duomo,* whose tallest spire, seemed to thrust defiantly into the sky the miraculous golden *Madonnina* of the Milanese. Would she also be hit? People were quickly coming out of their houses and making for the shelters. We eventually reached ours and started looking around for mother. She had already arrived and, in her relief at seeing us safe, she embraced us. This simple gesture reassured me so much that all fear left me. I settled down near her and started looking around. My attention was riveted by the sight of our neighbour who was sitting opposite daddy. She was a middle-aged woman, generally well-groomed and smartly dressed, with great poise and the most lovely fair hair, always perfectly combed and neatly arranged. Mother used to praise it in front of me, "Wouldn't you like to have hair like that when you grow up? Yours is so thin that you'll be bald before the age of forty," she would say every time she washed my hair. The hairwash ritual took place always against my will and was performed with a yoke of an egg to strengthen it and was followed by a rinse of camomile infusion to keep it fair.

But now our poor neighbour was certainly not a sight to be admired, shaking and bent double with fear and oblivious of everything but the danger of death, she was revealing for all the world to see a completely bald head! I looked first at mother and then at daddy; there was an unmistakable twinkle in his eyes when he slowly took his handkerchief out of his pocket and handed it to me to dry my eyes. I was crying with the effort of trying to suppress my irresistible laughter.

Just before we left Milan for the countryside my great-aunt Elena was suddenly carried off by emphysema. She was quite old by then, but she died as the eccentric she had always been. In her last years she had been an embarrassment and a worry to my parents because of the outspoken way she was in the habit of describing members of the government; often and gladly she would express her opinion about people who ruled us to whoever cared to listen. "Siamo governati da un branco di delinquenti" (We are ruled by a bunch of bandits), she would say quite loudly. And people did listen and once or twice they came to daddy to complain and to warn him about the unpleasant consequences of having such a candid aunt. But she went on undeterred, making fun of the most sacred tenets of what she called the police state, knowing that at her age nobody would dare to harm her. "Let them put me into jail," she would tell father when he tried to calm her down. "Ah, I would like that! I would die a martyr of the Fascists!"

She still lived with a companion in her rambling house in the

Aunt Elena

country, surrounded by her dogs, cats and pet parrot. My parents and I were with her when she died. She was propped up in bed by a great quantity of pillows and lace cushions and she had great difficulty in breathing. Her room, full of bric-a-brac and photographs, was dark and stuffy. There was a faint smell of age about. I stood there by her bed terrified by the death-rattle as she was gasping for air while daddy held her hand.

This was the first time I actually watched someone die and it was much worse than the shock I had when I saw Maria's body lying composed on her deathbed. Much more disturbing and horrifying. But she went peacefully and when it was all over a little smile crept over her face. The violence of my reaction to her death surprised my parents and mother had to give me some valeriana to quieten me down. I was also sincerely sorry to see her go and I cried inconsolably for the next two days.

In her will she left her money to trustees with the expressed wish that they should use it to look after her numerous pets. Her companion was to be given a yearly legacy provided she agreed to stay in the house and care for them. Afterwards the property should be turned into a kind of hostel for distressed animals.

I was left all her jewellery which was lovely and had some important pieces in it. Unfortunately, except for a few which we were lucky enough to be able to keep, we had to sell all, piece by piece, soon after the end of the war.

Aunt Elena was the last of my father's close relations. In fact, apart from my parents, from then on I didn't seem to have any kind of relative left anywhere in the world.

The village where we moved to escape from the bombardments wasn't far from Monza, then a smallish northern town of little interest except for the large industrial compound next to it which attracted regular bombing. Fortunately the village was on the other side of the town, and apart from a few occasions when some stray bombs fell on open fields nearby, we had no cause for fear.

Contessa Rossi, a friend of my mother's, lived in the manor house, a lovely villa built in the late eighteenth century, with a vast estate attached to it. We settled ourselves into a cottage in the grounds and we were to remain there for about two years until the Germans commandeered the property and had us all moved out.

Contessa Rossi was very rich. She was a widow who surrounded herself with brothers, sisters, cousins and a secretary, plus some nephews and nieces who came with their children to stay on and off during the summer months. There was a strong family resemblance among them; old and young, rich and poor, they all sported a large, hooked nose and had a tendency to get fat. They were short in size and temper. They had led different lives which had them scattered around the world and only the war had brought them temporarily together under the same roof. They made up an extraordinary group.

As we visited her almost every evening and spent hours in her company, the countess loved to tell us in great detail the story of her life and of the various members of her family. Despite her riches and her way of life she struck me as a rather pathetic figure. She had become a widow soon after her marriage, and had lost her only son during the First World War. For years after his death, she had pretended to herself that he would come back some day. She had kept his room ready for him, his clothes and shoes were neatly arranged in his wardrobe. Fresh flowers were put on a table near his ivory brushes. An old discoloured photograph of his fiancée in a long, lace gown still stood on his writing-table although the girl had long since married somebody else. For quite a few years after his death, the maid was ordered to prepare his bed and take a jug of water and a glass up to his room every night. His place at the head of the dining table, opposite his mother, was also laid down for him at every meal. However, by the time we went to live near her, this had been stopped, but the bedroom was still as he had left it some twenty-five years before.

Countess Rossi had a sweet tooth which put her often into trouble because she suffered from diabetes. She had a superb cook, a man from the village who had been in her service for years. One of my keenest memories of the period is the truly magnificent cakes he would make with stuff bought on the black market and with home-made jams. She had a love/hate relationship with him. Every morning he would ask her approval of his menu for the day but if she dared to suggest some changes he would accuse her of not trusting his judgement. A quarrel would follow and in the heat of the moment he would threaten to resign. The mere thought of losing his delicate soufflés and sublime Mont Blanc would have kept her awake at night, and so, in no time at all, she would make it up with him. If she was particularly pleased about a dish she would show her appreciation by summoning him to her study and, in a sudden, but not long-lasting impulse of democratic solidarity, she would shake hands with him!

Her brother was a bachelor and a retired diplomat who bored everyone with his stories about his days in Turkey and his love for a beautiful Turkish princess he had wanted to marry. But her father had sent his *janizaries* after him, threatening to kill him if he didn't leave her alone and in the end he had to run away. He kept a silver tear-catcher (a small vase with a top), which, he claimed, was full to the brim with the tears of the princess. Nobody really believed him but when he showed it to me I was really greatly impressed.

One of Countess Rossi's sisters, who had been married to a Spanish nobleman, had a daughter, Carmen, who first married a German and then ran away with another. Carmen herself had a son in the German army and a daughter married to an Englishman. Then there was the cousin who had married a Jew and, therefore, in deadly fear of the Nazis. Carmen was forever quarrelling with everybody and her standard reply to anyone who dared to express an opinion was a resounding *Jamais de la vie* (never in your life). They spoke to each other in Italian, French, German and Spanish indifferently and according to the mood they were in. I was told not to pick my nose in English and it was suggested rather vaguely by one of the old ladies that I should take up piano lessons as a way of keeping my fingers busy and away from my nose. My mother, not to be left out, told me that if I wanted to spend a penny, I should inform her with the statement *je vais faire un petit tour* and in the case of something more substantial *je vais faire un grand tour!* Feet were called the extremities and a bra *un soutien-gorge*. Carmen went about without a *soutien* although she had ample *gorge*.

During most of the year I was the only young person around and all those old souls took an interest in me and set about improving my general education. One began to give me painting lessons, the other to teach me the scales and they quarrelled over whether I should learn German or Spanish. German won and Carmen, in spite of her name, offered to teach it. Then Countess Rossi decided to make an elegant young thing out of me and got her maid to make me some dresses. They were terrible and I refused to wear them. Endless quarrels ensued with mother who felt I should wear them anyway, not to disappoint her friend.

But I was only a diversion to them because what they really loved doing was gambling. Not being able to go to Monte Carlo or Biarritz, *faute de mieux*, they organised chemin de fer and poker tables. I was taught how to play cards and invited to play with them to make up the number. Mother, of course, disapproved intensely of this type of teaching and no one could induce her to let me play for money. In the end they reached a compromise: they would be playing, as usual, for high stakes and I would be playing for love. My winning chips would be converted into money they said, and given to me on my eighteenth birthday. "Four years from now!" I protested to no avail. It seemed an eternity!

In the first year of my stay in that part of the country I was sent to a private school in Monza. It was a convent. The nuns were narrow-minded, jealous of each other, bossy and made the lives of their pupils incredibly difficult. I wondered about these nuns who were continually preaching obedience to us and who had to submit themselves to it as a rule of their lives. What a tremendously demanding vocation that was! Generally speaking, being told to do something had the immediate effect of making me not want to do it, and the more I was ordered about, the more I resisted. One should do a thing out of love and not out of obedience, I argued with them. And how many discussions we had! Sometimes I would go home and continue my argument with father. And once he suggested that, perhaps, as a way to learn, and as a punishment for my disobedience and because of my horror of cold weather in this present life, I would be reincarnated in my next one as a soldier of the Red Army stationed in Siberia. God forbid!

This problem of obedience was always with me; as far back as my mind would go I could recollect tension, tantrums and rages connected with my refusal to do as I was told. I remembered first La Fraulein ordering me about and then mother; now it was the nuns and my teachers. What I resented most was the arbitrary nature of their orders and prohibitions which, it seemed to me, were given without a reason. Why should I suddenly stop playing, perhaps when I was most enjoying myself, or go to sleep when I was wide awake? Why should I be nice to old Mrs. X and let her kiss me and smear my cheek with her disgusting lipstick and, worse still, prickle me with her moustache? Why must I do certain things and not others? The most infuriating thing was that I was never given a sensible explanation for their dictatorial behaviour. Now that I was a teenager and thought of myself as quite grown up, I beat my head against a wall of even more unreasonable prohibitions. I wasn't allowed to read most of Countess Rossi's large and well-furnished library because some books were not suitable for me. If I insisted to be allowed to chose for myself mother would soon lose her patience and complain that I was unbearable and stubborn. I was discouraged from walking around Monza by myself, to speak to strangers, to talk at the dining-table if we had guests and, worst of all, I would be sent out of a room if the grown-ups were talking about politics or if they were discussing some juicy bits of gossip about someone I knew. They would stop in the middle of a sentence if they noticed my presence among them and I was asked to go for a walk in the garden or to my room and work. "Run along, Clementina," they would say, "This conversation is not for you." How rude they were! Later, of course, towards the end of the war, the Germans did their bit by plastering all over the place placards, notices, posters with *verboten* written all over them.

I reacted to all this violently. When I was a child I would express my anger by screaming or by throwing myself to the floor and resist with all the weight of my body their unexplained dictates. Now I would be seized by an uncontrollable burst of tears and throw myself on the bed and hide my face in the pillows. How unfair it all was! I would tell myself between sobs, I shall run away some day and *then* they'll be sorry!

I had temporarily become very religious and often I would slip into the school chapel and ask God to make clear to me the reasons for this obvious injustice but, perhaps because I mostly went there to complain about it, my questions remained without an answer!

The nuns were, of course, a major source of grievance as they were the first to insist on obedience and modesty. They insisted that we wore our skirts so long that they almost swept the floor, that we pushed our hair well away from the forehead (little fringes or curls were considered too frivolous), and that we wore long sleeves even in summer. Slowly it dawned on me that not only children could be stupid but also some of the grown-ups. So now they could not only be boring but also stupid; it was stupid to attach so much importance to the outward appearance; it was also stupid of some teachers to praise Mussolini as our greatest hero when I knew from my father that it wasn't so; it was stupid of them to believe that I swallowed all the fibs they were telling me. Not being able to express my discontent in any sensible way, I remonstrated by being unruly during lessons and at the end of the second term I was given *zero in condotta* (zero mark in good behaviour) which was really quite serious. My parents were outraged and mother went to talk with the Mother Superior. The outcome of their conversation was that I would be sent to learn how to sew after school hours. This task was supposed to have a calming effect on me and, in the company of the nuns and the novices, I would learn the much needed virtues of stillness and discipline. So until the end of the school year I spent two hours every afternoon mending, darning and making hems while we recited the Rosary and the Litanies: *Mater purissima, Mater castissima, Mater inviolata, Mater intemerata, Ora pro nobis. Amen.*

I stuck to it till the end although it was so bitterly cold in their rooms that my fingers, stiff and full of chilblains, could hardly put the thread into the eye of the needle. But I knew when I was beaten and I certainly didn't want to repeat a full school year on account of some boring and stupid people!

Among our many duties at school we had to go to mass before lessons and to confession once a week. I was perhaps a bit immature and naive and sex hadn't as yet troubled me. Confession was an eye-opener. There was the priest, lurking darkly on the other side of the metal grate asking me whether I looked at boys, whether I took my bath naked and, worst of all, what did I do with my hands at night? These and other much more personal questions intrigued me so much that my imagination was fired off in various directions each week. Soon I consulted with the other girls and in a very short time, thanks to him, I lost my mental virginity.

As a way to insure that I wasn't going to be sent back to the convent for the next school year, one day I told father about some of the questions put to me by my Father Confessor. Daddy, never a practising Catholic, took a really dim view of the way his little girl's innocence had been perturbed. As my tale became more and more dramatic with more than a little exaggeration here and there, he changed colour a few times, thundering about that so-and-so of a priest and threatening to go and hang him by his dog collar. Mother eventually calmed him down, pointing out that sooner or later I should have to know the facts of life; but the following year I was back in a state school!

So another year went by in which I was being educated in more ways than one. That year Mussolini was arrested and taken to a prison up in the mountains of the Gran Sasso in Abruzzo and later liberated by a dashing German officer, Skorzeny, who whisked him off in a small plane. General Badoglio in Rome, became premier of the government that overthrew Mussolini and signed an armistice with the allies. Mussolini himself, by then in the north of Italy, declared that that part of the country would now become the Republic of Salò, effectively splitting Italy in two.

This turned out to be a great tragedy because what had started as a conventional war against a foreign enemy became an ugly civil war and created an emormous problem in the minds of a great number of upright men who had sworn allegiance to their king and to Mussolini. Geographically the region where we lived belonged to the Fascist side, the Republican North. We were not under direct fire from the two fighting armies, but we had to cope with the continuous bombing and the increasing nastiness of the Fascist and German reprisals against partisan guerillas. Every time one German was killed ten civilians would be taken at random from the streets and shot, often on the spot. There was also for every man between eighteen and sixty years of age, the ever-present threat of being suddenly *rastrellato,* that is press-ganged and sent to the labour camps in Germany. On top of all this, there was, for a time, near starvation for everybody, the quantity of food allocated on the ration cards being simply derisory, if one managed to get any, after hours of queueing.

I lived intensely through these developments because of my father. The recurrence of his disease compelled him to give up any idea of working even in an office and he miserably stayed at home with us with bouts of beri-beri, this time crippling him in his arms. He would try to analyse and discuss with me the current political events, encouraging me to explore the depth of the human spirit and the autonomy of man's reason. But most of the time, sitting in his old leather armchair near the fireplace which, more often than not, had no crackling logs in it, he would read to me chapters from the Italian classics, poetry and history books. He had a wonderful voice and a great imagination. It was delightful to hear him recount episodes and battles about . . . . . wicked popes and saintly kings.

Father was very fond of eating frogs which, like the French, he considered a delicacy. To give him a little treat and to ensure at least a meal, I used to go to the stream which weaved its way through the property and, armed with a bucket which I would cover with a piece of cloth, I would catch frogs by hand and throw them quickly into the bucket. So for that evening, at least, supper was guaranteed: *"Grenouilles frittes au riz."* Mother would say contentedly "Anche per oggi abbiamo mangiato" (for today we have been fed).

Mother tried her best to feed us and she spent a lot of time preparing dishes using her ingenuity to make them look like the real thing. For example, she made some omelettes with non-existing eggs using an evil-smelling yellowish powder. The roast beef was made with horse-meat and we suspected that *le lapin à la chinoise* might have been an unlucky cat because her butcher gave her pieces of rabbit already sliced and cleaned and one couldn't be sure to whom these cuts had originally belonged. She would bake cakes made with mashed carrots and sweet potatoes and mixed with some greyish flour which looked revolting; the bread was also grey and now and then she would secure some equally revolting cheese. But she was a good cook and I gulped down everything which was put in front of me with great relish because I was always hungry.

I also had the bad habit of putting all sorts of things into my mouth especially leaves, flowers and resins and I could recommend the flowers of the wistaria and the resins of most fruit trees, which I found delicious.

One of my chief pleasures was to wander in the huge park which surrounded Countess Rossi's villa or cycle on the narrow sandy paths which divided the fields of the now disused farm. During the summer months I would get up early and run barefoot on the lawn which was still wet with dew. The early sunrays would tint the purple beeches and the silvery poplars which lined the drive of the villa. I would go down to the stream, past the weeping willows and wade through it, watching the tadpoles scatter away in fear. Later in the day I might take a book with me and lie on a hammock. Pretending to read, I would listen to the sounds of the summer from the hum of the bees and the buzz of the wasps to the chatter of the birds and the whispering of the leaves. I would recite aloud to myself some poetry about the beauty of nature and the sight of the swallows darting in the sky would fill my eyes with tears. It was obvious that I was becoming very romantic—a state of affairs that only a few months before I would have considered the height of stupidity.

I was going through a difficult period having just become, with a certain amount of shock and pain, what mother called "a little woman". I had also began to look at myself with attention and with a critical eye and I didn't like what I saw. My hair was too

Reading in the hammock

straight and yellow, my mouth too big, my legs too bony and my chest too flat. Nothing about me looked good except, perhaps, my nose of which I was extremely proud, believing it to be a perfect Greek nose. But that wasn't really enough to make me attractive or irresistible. Some of the grown-ups had complimented me on my looks and one of the old ladies up at the villa had said to my father that "Clementina deviendra une fille charmante", but I didn't believe them at all. Mother, overworked and short of money, didn't take much trouble with my clothes and not wanting to give me the wrong ideas would go out of her way to criticise my looks, my posture, my *gaucherie*, saying that I looked more like a young donkey than a young filly and I, for once, sadly agreed with her.

Another cause of my restlessness and dissatisfaction, although I couldn't recognise it at the time, was that, having been given to read masses of books which were supposed to be suitable reading for young ladies and which were, in fact, idiotic romantic novels, I would gorge myself on them and dream of being a stunning beauty surrounded by love-smitten young men. But, unfortunately, in real life I had to content myself with the boys of my school who were uninteresting young brutes, still in their shorts, and full of pimples and eczema, whose erotic dreams, when they had any, would be sparked by florid maidens and sexy pin-up girls, but never by skinny me. So I invented a Prince Charming who would be smitten by my Twiggy figure, ask for my hand and make me ecstatically happy ever after. In the meantime I brooded and ate pounds of indigestible bread in the hope of developing my unripe figure!

The temperature during the winter months fell well below zero and I suffered from the cold abominably. There was no way to warm the cottage except by burning logs in the fireplace and in the kitchen stove. But it was extremely difficult to find any. Even the benches had been taken away from public parks by people in need of some wood to burn. The foresters had come too, to cut down the beautiful old trees and the young ones. The noise of their saws was deafening and heart-breaking: it was very sad to watch those tall trees being felled and infuriating to know that none of their wood would be coming our way. Everything was for "them", the Germans.

German soldiers were everywhere. Tall, fair and arrogant, but also lonely. Some would try to stop us schoolgirls in the streets for the sake of a smile and a little chat. They went around armed to the teeth but also carrying photographs of their families which they tried to show us.

At my school there were some Jewish girls who, after a few months of attendance, had to stop coming because of the pressure put on them and the veiled threats made by the Fascists; others had to escape to Switzerland. I knew of the brothers of some of my school-friends who were sent to labour camps in Germany, and some others who took to the mountains where they joined partisan groups.

I was much happier at the state school where I mixed with young people of different backgrounds and interests, people I never had the chance to meet before, like the children of working-class families or the middle-classes of a small provincial town. No doubt, by sending me to the convent the previous year, my parents, and my mother in particular, had tried to shelter me from just this type of encounter which, according to her, was full of unspecified dangers. For my mother it was essential to keep one's place in society and if one was lucky enough to be born into the upper-classes one should stick to them and therefore mix only with one's own sort.

From this sprang her usual insistence in wanting to know the surnames of my favourite school-friends. So when I asked her permission to bring Laura, one of the girls, home for tea, I had to go through a barrage of questions which was in no way inferior to the notorious Spanish Inquisition. Who were her parents? What was her name? Where did she live? What was her father doing?

Laura's surname meant nothing to her and it was quickly dismissed with a curt "never heard of it" which by itself was a reproof; when I told her that Laura's father was a haberdasher and had a shop in the main street she almost fainted! But then hearing that Laura's mother was half Jewish and, therefore, that they were all in some danger, my mother, who was always kind-hearted in spite of all her snobbishness, promptly agreed to meet her. "By all means, bring your new friend home," she said, "The poor child! I can well imagine what a difficult time she must go through."

And so it was. Her family lived in continual fear but, having a cousin who was a high official in the Fascist government of the republic, they had decided to stay on in Monza in the hope that, if the need arose, he would be able to shelter them from eventual reprisal.

Laura was two years older than I. She was a classical Italian beauty, taller than I and altogether more mature. Her figure was fully developed and her dark eyes had already a depth of understanding which was unusual in one so young; they were also sad. She was one of a large family which seemed to be very close-knit and well-integrated. They were great music lovers and they all knew how to play some kind of instrument. Often they would get together after a meal and perform with great talent and precision some pieces of classical music.

I loved to visit them and they surrounded me with kind attention; Laura's mother was a pleasant, friendly woman who always welcomed me with a cheerful smile. Her father insisted on calling me *signorina*, but often made appreciative remarks about my dimples; a thing which endeared him to me enormously! So when I got home with Laura that afternoon for tea I was a bit nervous not knowing how my mother would receive her. But I shouldn't have worried as she was at her most charming and sweet self and had even made a kind of strawberry cake for us.

This was the beginning of a lasting friendship which gave us both a lot of pleasure and comfort in the years to come. Laura was a quiet, highly intelligent girl and I admired her immensely. She seemed to know already what she wanted from life and she had made up her mind to go to university and become a doctor. She used to talk to me about her love for humanity and her desire to help it. She could play the piano quite nicely and she used to practise for hours on end. She lent me some books which we would then discuss together. They were mostly serious books about the great western philosophers and I found them hard going but, of course, I would have died rather than let her suspect that I had some difficulties in finishing them and run the danger to be told again, as she had done once before, that "there was a superficial side of me which we must keep under control." She was right, of course, as I still liked best of all to have fun, to go to the cinema, to talk about romantic love and to have a lot of giggles. Laura instead was very serious, romance didn't interest her a little bit and she seldom laughed; perhaps she was a little too eager and tense to be able to develop a sense of humour which was one of the few things lacking in her otherwise almost perfect character.

One day as we were sitting around the kitchen table in her house, the doorbell rang three times in quick succession as for a signal, and moments later a young man walked into the kitchen. He was slightly built with a mane of long hair and an intense manner. His name was Michele and I learnt later that he was a partisan. He was nineteen, very full of himself, but probably also very afraid. He wore spectacles which was then quite unusual for young people, and they gave him the air of an intellectual. Michele was Laura's first cousin and when in Monza he would call at her house because he had no other place to go, his family having escaped to Switzerland the previous year. Instead of following them there he had decided to stay and join the underground movement because he said "I have seen too many homes wrecked, fathers and sons arrested, neighbours hurt and because I have a spirit of freedom in me which cannot be quenched." As I was already becoming fascinated by ideas of freedom, democracy and the daring exploits of some of the men up in the mountains, talk of which I heard in Laura's house, I couldn't help but be greatly impressed by Michele's rhetorical little speech. In fact I was bowled over by it or more accurately by *him*. In no time my mind was made up, I would become a partisan on the spot!

I was to see Michele quite often for the next week or two and his tales of heroism combined with his romantic personality made him quite irresistible in my eyes. It was the classic "crush". I realise now that he was probably putting it on in a big way to impress his uncle and, perhaps, to give himself confidence, but I listened spellbound to all he said and to his recital of obscure poems which he called beautiful without even explaining what they were all about! Unfortunately Michele didn't seem to notice my existence on this planet and to my greatest disappointment I realised that Michele's second main interest in life seemed to be food and he never seemed to have enough of it. But he must have noticed the adoring look on my face, despite his ostentatious attitude of complete indifference towards us girls—close friends of his cousin—because once, instead of walking past our little group with his nose in the air, ignoring us, as usual, he actually turned his head and called me aside. "Would you do something very important for me?" "Oh yes," I replied eagerly. *"Anything."* "Well then," Michele continued, "Go to the piazza at five o'clock and wait near the newspaper kiosk for a man who will give you a parcel. Have you got a red sweater? Good, wear it and he will understand that I sent you."

Bursting with pride and excitement, I did what I was told. At four-thirty I was already waiting near the kiosk. A man, after asking for my name, gave me a parcel. "It's for Michele," he said briefly and left. I could hardly contain my excitement. What could there be in it? A bomb? It didn't tick, though. Perhaps a gun or some stuff with which to blow up a bridge (partisans were forever blowing up bridges), or some secret documents? I ran all the way to Laura's home holding the precious parcel under one arm. "Well done, ragazzina, thanks," he said to me when I handed it over to him. *Ragazzina*, indeed! Rather hurt to be called "girlie" to my face at the end of my mission, I stood by and watched him untie the brown string with nervous fingers. Out of the parcel and out of the innumerable wrappers of old newspapers, emerged bare and ludicrous, three salami and four pairs of sausages!

Undaunted by this down-to-earth side of my hero, I continued to dream about future exciting incidents in which I could see myself saving lives here and there, snatching innocent victims from the SS just in the nick of time and hiding them, against the most dangerous odds! I was just waiting for the first opportunity to act; and, in the meantime, my practical way to help the cause was to give wrong directions to the Germans when they asked the way. To the background of giggles from my girl-friends, I would very seriously indicate the wrong turning, the wrong square, the wrong street to some harassed German driver. We would also take down some notices put up by the Germans. Most of them started with a huge *Achtung* followed by a list of things which were *Verboten* to the citizens. It became quite an obsession: the list got longer and longer and one could hardly walk any distance at all without finding one staring at you from a wall.

I resented very much all those *verboten* from the Germans and their Fascist friends, more than I ever resented any other prohibition. And I had been a notorious rebel all my life! But now my parents became rather worried about my enthusiasm for the partisan cause and kept me at home as much as possible. Laura was by now a most welcome guest at our house because mother had decided that she had a good influence on me. She saw her as a serious, steady and thoughtful girl who would put a break on my fanciful imagination and, most of all in the present situation, as a strong positive influence in discouraging me in my fervent desire to follow the partisans. Laura with her Jewish background, was far too sensible and scared to expose herself to the attention of the Germans by doing something foolish. But I wanted to become a real partisan, I wanted to go up to the mountains or go to Milan where people got killed either by the Allied bombing or by German reprisals. I wanted to make myself useful at the prisoner-of-war camp nearby, but most of all, I wanted to see Michele again, with his glasses and a red scarf around his neck. I wanted all sorts of things which were neither possible nor sensible but I could only express my frustration by sending Germans out of their way and by being generally difficult. It was about this time that mother began pitying the poor man who would marry me!

Then one day, as Laura and I were hiding, as we often did, with our books up on the branches of my favourite tree, we heard the sound of the siren of a car and, moments later, the screech of brakes. Peeping through the leaves we saw some German officers coming out of two cars, just outside the main entrance of the property. The gate-keeper had come quickly out of his lodge to open the gates and let them in and was told that they wished to go up to the villa and talk immediately with its owner. He asked them to wait while he announced them through the house-phone, and Laura and I climbed down our tree and dashed to the villa where we found the old ladies in a great state of agitation, alarmed as they were by the unexpected visit. They were all staunch royalists and therefore opposed to the Republic of Salò; what's more they often listened to the B.B.C. news and they were now afraid that one of the servants might have given them away. Countess Rossi finally received them in her little study and listened with mounting concern to their request. They said they had come to requisition her property as they planned to live in her villa and in the two cottages next to it. She and some of her relations would be allowed to stay on, possibly moving to a wing of the house if other suitable arrangements couldn't be made but, the officers insisted, everything had to be done fairly quickly. The countess was staggered but there was nothing she could do and she agreed to their request with the minimum fuss. So the poor old things— herself, her brother, sister, cousin, secretary and her precious cook, their lives thrown into confusion—scattered like frightened hens in all directions. Likewise we were told to move out of our cottage.

Where to go? Frantic searches on the part of my parents and finally we were told that we could go and stay in an empty castle near Novara.

I was very sorry to move away from Monza and much more, of course, to part from Michele and Laura. In fact I wasn't to see Michele again for many years and when we finally met in Laura's house he had become a successful and sedate businessman with a wife and three children and he had some difficulty in recalling who I was. But I kept in touch with Laura, from whom I had become inseparable. She would often write, with the precision proper to an accountant, about herself and her family which was to survive, unharmed at the end of the hostilities. Her Fascist cousin was eventually taken prisoner by the partisans at the very end of the war and, after a quick trial, shot for crimes committed against civilians.

We arrived at the castle late at night after a tedious and difficult journey made unbearably long by the frequent stops and controls of the republican guards. But a perfect moon was shining over it, illuminating with its pale rays the turrets and the drawbridge and the water of the moat which surrounded it. We had been met at the station by the agent who had come with a pony and trap to take us there and now, in spite of the weariness and fatigue of the trip, we couldn't but be impressed by the beauty and the charm of the place.

Next day I went through all the rooms to help mother and the agent's wife open the windows and take away the dust covers from the furniture. I admired the bedrooms with their four-poster beds which faintly smelled of moth-balls and camphor, the large drawing-rooms with their crystal chandeliers hanging from the high ceilings and, most of all, the wood-panelled study which led to a large library. Its four walls were lined from top to bottom with bookshelves. All the books were bound with red leather and on the first page of each book there was the coat of arms of its owner with *ex-libris* and his name written on it.

There was also an armoury and a room which had stuffed animals on its walls. "Who are these intruders?" they seemed to ask, their glass eyes peering down at us with a critical air. All the rooms smelled of age and neglect and, as one opened the shutters, one had the feeling of disturbing some hidden pattern and some bygone spirits. There was a kind of magic in the place as if time had stood still for over half-a-century.

But its greatest recommendation was that it was near a farm. It had become increasingly difficult to find food except, at times, on the black market, but the things one could get there were often too dear for us. I still remember a whole month in which we ate nothing but dry chestnuts and milk.

I settled down in these new surroundings cheerfully enough, not only because they were outstanding and bewitching but also because I was getting used to my gipsy life and I lived from day to day. It was then 1944 and the Allied troops were fighting their way up the shores of the Italian Peninsula and news of the German retreat was filtering through the Fascist censorship. Soon, we were hoping and praying, the war would be over!

In the meantime we made do with whatever we could find.

Luckily one of the farmer's sons, Mario, was a young seminarist who, soon after our arrival, escorted me round his father's farm. It was a large one and in spite of the frequent requisitions of the Fascists, it seemed to me quite rich. I looked wide-eyed at the cows in their stables, at the pigs and the poultry, even enjoying the smell of wet straw and cow manure!

In the dairy I was dazzled by the sight of glazed earthenware, wooden barrel-churns and assorted pots containing butter and soft cheeses which were covered with white gauze. Up in the loft, fruit was stored and ripened on wide planks, and the silkworms, on their mulberry leaves, were busy at their work. The next room had strings of sausages, ropes of onions, bacon and large hams hanging from hooks in the ceiling and cupboards full of green bottles containing tomato sauce and jams; on its floor rested large sacks of flour and rice—such abundance took my breath away!

The seminarist was a strange young man. Although he walked about with his prayer-book devoutly open, he didn't seem to read it much and, coming back from school, I would find him waiting for me with a bunch of violets hidden in his cassock. Often and in great secret, he would add to the flowers some eggs and sometimes even a chicken or two. In the summer during the hot afternoons when the stillness of the countryside was only broken by the noise of a hornet or a cicada, he would lazily sit by me on the grass and we would talk. He could be lyrical about the colours of the changing sky and the reds and purples and violets of the sunset. He would use phrases like "the sun lavishing its caresses on me" and "the wind whirling around my golden hair". I went along with all this talk because I had developed a most romantic love for the countryside and I would ask him what he thought about nature and the theory of evolution. He didn't seem to be much interested in either. In fact, he seemed much more interested in human nature and mine in particular, than in Nature with a capital N.

I must add that I was briefly going through "my Rousseau period" which I immediately disowned when I discovered Voltaire, but at the time, I dreamt of living in the country on the good earth and away from the pollution of a big city. And I was still in my heroic-romantic mood which had began when I had met Michele. When I was inflamed with his patriotic ardour my head had been full of the heroic feats I would have shared with him in the mountains. Every time I had climbed up a tree and settled myself comfortably on a strong forking branch with a book in my hand and a good resolution to do some work, my imagination had carried me away to his side, and I had pictured myself dressed in trousers and sheepskin coat, with a machine-gun across my shoulder, laying ambushes and helping capture German soldiers, in short, becoming a kind of female Pimpernel.

However, in the meantime, I was keenly aware of Mario's attentions and I began wondering whether I was seducing him away from God for the sake of a few sausages. My father was also keeping a keen and suspicious eye on him while mother seemed quite content to receive his generous provisions. It eventually transpired that his love for the church was mainly inspired by his fear of the Fascists on the one hand and his hesitation to go and rough it with the partisans on the other!

I realise that in setting out to describe my romantic period, invariably I end up with talks about food: this is because when I go back in my mind to the last period of the war, I find that food or the lack of it, had an overwhelming importance in my life. I might have believed that to be interesting a girl had to be ethereal and pale (the lean and hungry look, I suppose) and starved to the point of nearly fainting, but the real truth was that I couldn't resist a plate of spaghetti, unromantic as it might be. I might have cried reading Leopardi's *Infinito* but I would eat the spaghetti nevertheless, tears running down my cheeks at the sadness of the poem. The real trouble was that there were not enough of them!

I must have spent all my teenage years in a world of make-believe. I invented a situation and identified myself with a part in it: a heroine, a princess, a saint, and I would move, dress, or talk accordingly. The same character could last quite a long time before a new one would take its place. My romantic period was eventually substituted with that of the sophisticated woman. Without once having seen or heard of Greta Garbo, I decided that to be sophisticated meant behaving in a distant, detached sort of way; I wanted to be alone. Sitting with my friends with a far-away look in my eyes and trying not to say a word, I would sigh and say that I was so tired because I spent the whole night reading Sartre or Nietzche or Schopenhauer, and often actually doing so. I pretended to be a lot bored and a little cynical about everything and everybody. As I was naturally very fond of laughing and teasing and a chatterbox to boot, this new impersonation presented quite a few difficulties. It lasted, in fact, only a short time mostly because of my father's pitiless imitation of my snobbish, sophisticated self. He would imitate my imitation of a sophisticated woman, my newly-found affected way of speaking, and make fun of my pallor and black circles under my eyes which were made darker by gently brushing carbon paper over them. So I dropped sophistication and I embraced life in the service of others. I would become a doctor; working to the limit of my capability to save human lives, I would be praised by all as a woman Doctor Schweitzer, perhaps even going to Africa to cure leprosy. And that wasn't all: I considered taking a double degree in medicine and veterinary science so that I could cure just about everybody in the two kingdoms! When the right time came, I even applied to the University of Medicine!

I felt sure that somebody would eventually leave me a great deal of money. It had to be someone incredibly old, whom I, for once, couldn't snatch away from death but whom I helped to die in peace from old age after weeks of dedicated nursing. I would distribute this money to all the people who needed it. It would be done anonymously, perhaps by sending it in an envelope with a typed note explaining that I was repaying an old debt, or perhaps that it was just a gift from God. Nobody would ever know that it came from me and everybody would be happy and believe that life was fair and just. As a matter of fact I personally couldn't understand why rich people didn't do that sort of thing anyway. It would be lovely, I thought, if a nice old gentleman, seeing me admiring a perfectly beautiful sapphire necklace in the shop-window of Cartier's, would address me and say: "Do you really like it? Then, do me the honour of accepting it from me." And so saying he would enter the shop and buy it. Then handing me the little parcel wrapped up in golden paper and lifting his hat in a farewell greeting, he would cross the road and disappear around the corner! Why not? After all, I would have liked to do the same sort of things myself if I had the money.

Then I discovered asceticism. I plunged into it with all the enthusiasm of a neophyte and I decided to become a holy person. I vowed I would meditate every day, stop eating meat and never drink another drop of wine for the rest of my life. As this followed immediately the short-lived glamorous girl period, it came as a surprise to all. I stopped wearing make-up and curling my hair and dressed very simply. Indeed, I almost succeeded in controlling my quick temper and went about smiling angelically to everybody. Even to strangers in the streets, shops and buses. This behaviour caused more than a misunderstanding with some of the male population who, too obtuse to see my growing aura and luminous radiations, misinterpreted my beatific smiles. But I was undeterred. "I shall go through life spreading love and good will; that would be my mission!" I would often repeat this resolution to myself and to anyone who cared to listen.

But I am running ahead of the events which were shaking our part of the country. While Southern and Central Italy were slowly being liberated by the Allied troops, the North was still the stronghold of Mussolini's Republic of Salò. The Germans had felt betrayed after what they called Badoglio's treachery, meaning his surrender to the Allies of the Italian armies back in 1943 and now that the tide of the war was turning against them they were increasingly harassed by the various anti-Fascist movements which had sprung up right from the beginning, but which recently had become more organised. The partisans were indeed blowing up bridges and throwing bombs and fast becoming effective in guerilla warfare. Ghastly stories began to circulate about concentration camps in which it was whispered that not only Jews but also other people had been deliberately starved to death, and we heard endless rumours about vicious German reprisals. In fact, more proclamations were glued to the walls of the towns announcing that from now on the reprisals for Germans killed or wounded would be extended to the terrorists' families: the men would be shot and their families deported. The republican newspapers unleashed furious rhetoric against the partisans calling them "these murderers who sabotaged their own country", or words of that kind. It really was like a civil war. Over it all the R.A.F. sent us bombers which, like God who sends His rain on the just and the unjust, impartially destroyed buildings, blew up military targets and railway stations and occasionally, like in my case, tried to kill romantic young girls. This came about because my new school was in Novara a few miles away from the castle and I used to cycle there and back every morning. I loved the ride through the lovely country lanes which divided the rice fields from the woodlands. The last stretch was on the main road leading into town and near a railway junction. That last bit was fairly dangerous because of the Allies' habit of flying above it and machine-gunning anything that moved.

One day, on my way back home, I saw a British plane high in the sky and approaching very quickly from the opposite direction. The road was deserted except for a lorry carrying rice and two peasants following it on bicycles. One of the cyclists and I threw ourselves into a nearby ditch and, to our horror, watched the plane diving fast on to the road and opening fire. In no time at all it was gone, leaving three people dead, the two men in the lorry and the other cyclist.

So much were we conditioned to these happenings after four years of war, that I got hold of my bicycle and continued my trip home, where I didn't say a word about the incident to my parents. I was afraid they wouldn't let me move about any more. And just as well, the same plane came back again and again regularly, hardly missing a day. Only its timetable changed. We called it Pippo.

The second time Pippo tried to interfere with my life, I wasn't so lucky. It was early morning and I was cycling towards Novara when I saw it coming down fast towards me. I took shelter under a small bridge leaving my bicycle on the road. Pippo saw a car approaching and promptly opened fire before disappearing in the sky, a small black dot against the sun.

The driver of the car was only slightly wounded, but his car and my bicycle had been badly damaged. We sat at the edge of the road waiting for help and soon a hearse passed by and stopped. It was on its way to the graveyard and it was carrying a coffin. We got in the back of the van and sat by the side of the coffin among wreaths and bunches of flowers until we reached the town where I got off near my school.

This new encounter with Pippo couldn't be hidden from my parents and for more than a week I was kept at home. Eventually as the end of the school year and the exams were approaching, it was agreed to let me resume my daily journeys to school but I had to promise to take a slightly longer way by which I could avoid the main road. I was very keen to attend, so as not to be left behind with my work. But if I went to school every day and in the end passed my exams, I did it all in an absent-minded sort of way because I was becoming increasingly attentive to politics and to the struggles which were going on. If I had become a partisan on the spot as a childish reaction to my crush for Michele, now I wanted to choose my side with my mind as well.

Hearing all those rumours about German atrocities, in the beginning I had been perplexed and amazed. I just couldn't believe that those tall blond chaps with their pink complexions, who showed us the photographs of their families and spoke so politely in their broken Italian could be responsible for such actions. The didn't look so cruel; in fact I couldn't believe that anybody could be so cruel.

Until quite recently I had known nothing about politics. I disliked the Fascists mainly because I saw them through daddy's eyes to begin with and then through those of people like Michele. I remembered reading a story, a few years before, in our text book at school about a small boy who had been offered a reward for having passed his exams with top marks. He was given the choice of going to Rome to meet his Duce or of acquiring a brand new bicycle. To my great amazement, the boy chose to go to Rome and I judged him an incredible cretin. But I had left it at that and it didn't occur to me to pass judgement on a leader who wanted little boys to believe that he was better than a bicycle.

Now I began putting hard questions to my father, my teachers and listening to the talks of the farm-hands and in the shops where mother often sent me on various errands and I began to understand the struggle and the rage which so evidently divided the country.

Soon I was going to be convinced. I discussed my earlier perplexities with Laura who had come to visit us for a few days.

I remember going to the station to meet her train. The waiting-room was packed with troops and civilians loaded with parcels and suitcases. I sat down on a corner of a wooden bench near the glass window and watched the trains go by. A sealed train passed through without stopping, it was full of men on their way to the labour camps in Germany. Would they ever come back I wondered? A little later another train arrived and the troops boarded it; now there were only civilians left on the platform. Laura's train was late, and when it finally pulled in, it was so crowded that it was almost impossible to get the carriage doors open. A burly man eventually managed to disengage them and Laura got off. I hadn't seen her for almost a year and we looked at each other with curiosity. She had changed and grown thinner. She was more beautiful than ever, moving and walking with a light graceful gait; she seemed to have definitely emerged from the awkward age, and her face had become really lovely under her smooth dark hair. As we walked away from the platform, people were looking at her but she went by seemingly unaware of the sensation she was creating. "She must have grown used to it," I thought, "Lucky thing!" "Let's go to the bar and have something to drink"—she asked presently, "I'm dying of thirst."

We made our way through the crowd and went into *il bar della stazione* where we ordered some soft drinks. Guards patrolled the place, rifles on shoulders, but we couldn't find out why. The large bar was packed and we had to stand near the counter. Some Italian travellers, tired and shabby-looking, sat around the tables munching a little snack or dozing off waiting for the next train, surrounded by children and parcels. They contrasted vividly with the Germans who sat in large groups by themselves, well-groomed and even cheerful. They came and went and saluted with the usual clicking of heels, while others were eating and drinking some beer. When Laura dropped her purse a German officer got up politely to pick it up for her. I remember being surprised by the look of contempt in her eyes when she almost snatched it away from him. Immediately afterwards she got up and we made our way to the square to ride home in the farmer's pony and trap with which I had come to meet her.

That night, lying on our beds, the lights out, we talked for hours; there was so much to catch up and to discuss. I quickly realised that Laura had something really important to tell me. Some months before—she began—her fear for her own safety and that of her family had given away to a great desire to do something against what she now called the oppressors. I could hear in her voice her resentment and hate against those people who had deported and perhaps killed some of her mother's relations. With her change of heart, came the resolve to join what she now called the cause, and she had left her parents and gone up to the mountains with Michele. I was out of myself with curiosity and admiration and also a little envy. How lucky she was! I bombarded her with questions: "Where are you staying?" "What do you do there?" "Are you actually carrying a gun?" Laura, of course, wouldn't answer any of my questions pleading the oath of secrecy she had made. "But can I join you?" I asked rather rashly, knowing perfectly well that my parents would never allow me to go. She didn't seem so keen on the idea herself but she volunteered to say that she had brought with her some pamphlets which she wanted me to distribute around Novara. "Would you do it for us?" she asked, and added cunningly—"It's really Michele who sent them, you know." Michele! How could I refuse.

Laura only stayed with us for a week-end and I took her around the property and the farm, stressing the bliss of country-life. "Yes, of course, if you happen to live in a castle," she remarked rather tartly. Naturally she showed her greatest scorn for poor Mario, that *mezzo prete* (half priest) as she called him and wouldn't accept even a teeny-weeny sausage from him. We were all very impressed by her beauty and self-confidence and my unsuspecting mother praised her once more for being so sensible and mature. "You see, Clementina," she added comparing me unfavourably to her, "Why can't you grow up too?" which, under the circumstances was rather ironical. Laura left to go back to her hills and dangerous life leaving behind a bunch of badly cyclostyled papers which I hid under my mattress.

For a time, every morning, I took a few of them and hid them in my bra before cycling to Novara and distributing them around as I had been told. Naturally, my parents were mercifully and completely in the dark about these extra-curricula activities of mine and never suspected anything. Only once or twice my mother remarked favourably about my sudden tidiness when she found out that I was now making up my bed very promptly every morning!

My parents and I enjoyed living in the castle and father had begun to feel better; he could walk almost normally now and had been asked by its owner to supervise the property. He went around in a pony and trap, often taking me along with him. Months went by, monotonous in their precariousness and uncertainty of the future. Then the spring of 1945 was with us and the whole atmosphere around us changed. Rumours of the German retreat multiplied while the official news about the widely publicised miraculous breakthrough, Hitler's secret weapon, the V2, petered out. The press, the radio, and even Mussolini's speeches had now a different tone. They would warn us about the terrible evils which would befall us if Germany was defeated. Father was quick to notice the change and he remarked that until quite recently, it had been considered a serious offence to express such a conjecture even in private. Perhaps this meant that we were at last nearing the end of the struggle. We lived in suspended animation a little longer and then, at long last, it was all over!

I had got up at the very last minute, that morning, and I was cycling down my usual way towards the town when, reaching the main road I met a German column going in the opposite direction. They marched in step and looked straight ahead; behind them came tanks, trucks and artillery. One could hear a distant rumble of guns and the rat-tat-tat of machine-gun fire. I went on and soon all roads were thick with traffic. Along one I saw an overturned tank and some burnt-out vehicles, then more and more people. "There has been an uprising," they were saying, "They are pulling out." I looked around, more Germans were coming in my direction shouting orders in their guttural language and loud military voices. What was going on? The volleys of the tommy-guns could be heard more clearly, but the swastika was still flying from the flag-pole of a building.

I managed to reach the school on foot, pushing my bicycle along. There I found a few of my class-mates. A boy shouted at me, "It's over, it's over! The partisans are blowing up German trucks, the railway workers are sabotaging their trains. Evviva, evviva!" I was caught by the general excitement and with a couple of other girls I walked around the streets just to see what was happening.

It seemed that everybody else had the same idea and the throng of people was pressing on us, giving us a sense of suffocation. Some women were laughing, others crying and everybody was out of control. My head began to spin. We sat on the steps of a church and watched the crowd which was suddenly waving thousands of *tricolore,* the Italian flag. The air seemed overcharged with electricity; hours went by, it was late afternoon now and it was becoming dark. The noise of the guns in the distance had softened down. The two girls set off towards their houses and I went back to the school looking for my bicycle. It wasn't there. Somebody must have borrowed it. How was I to go home? I felt exhausted after the tremendous excitement of the long day and overcome by a mixture of feelings—bewilderment, exultation and fear.

I stood there, in front of the school gate, wondering what to do when I saw my father pushing his way through the crowd coming towards me and I ran, relieved, into his arms. I was safe . . . all of us were safe at last . . . the war was over!

Chapter Six

AFTERMATH

The end of the war meant different things to different people. If some of my school-friends were looking forward to the return of a father or a brother from a German labour camp or a prisoner-of-war camp in England and others were hoping to see their partisan relations again, to quite a few it represented disgrace and fear because their fathers had been officers of the Republic of Salò. But to all it meant the end of an impossible situation and most people greeted the Allied forces with all the joy and the relief one feels at the end of a nightmare.

Like the bewildered youth of the post-war period, I was also carried away by the general excitement and the high hopes one had for a better world with a better and more just society. Immediately after the end of the hostility, tremendous political activity took place and there were meetings and assemblies in the city squares, in the town halls and even in the schools. I attended a great number of them trying to make some sense out of the various forms of democracy suddenly offered to the Italian people.

One can have many different reasons for taking up a position when young, idealistic reasons mostly but also frivolous and romantic. Partly remembering the shy young man with spectacles who had become my hero and partly to spite my mother who was a staunch conservative, I decided to become a socialist. To show off my new-found identity I started wearing a red jumper, the only red item I owned and I only took it off to wash it when it was so dirty that its colour became a brownish hue; in that condition, of course, it would have been counter-productive: it had to be flaming red!

Suddenly all the fascists had disappeared. Women who had fraternised with them and the Germans had their hair shorn off. Every other person was a partisan. If it was quite impossible to prove that one had fought up in the hills with them, people would make you believe that secretly they had supported them all along.

The partisans themselves, went about looking very important with guns over their shoulders. Near where we lived many of them were communists or socialists and generally labelled *rossi* (reds), like Michele.

Allied soldiers were everywhere, distributing chewing-gum, cigarettes and candies and, to the *signorine* nylon stockings. The *signorine* were the same girls who had befriended the Germans but had been lucky enough not to have their hair shorn off. As my mother regarded them all as whores I defended them as being a product of the capitalistic system whereas, I felt sure, they were mostly and simply hungry. As I was still the most impressive greenhorn and consequently light years away from their world, I was greatly fascinated by them and their wicked ways.

Instead of signboards saying *achtung* and *verboten* we now had signs with *Off Limits*. Instead of the dour Germans we had cheerful and loud Americans and amusing British troops with lots of coloured men in their midst, Negroes, Indians, black Africans and Moroccans who might have come in with the French. I didn't know exactly who was who but the excitement ran high and I looked in amazement at all those foreigners. Some of my girl-friends who knew a little English showed off like mad talking with them in the streets. I was green with envy.

The air was full of new songs which, like many foreign films, had been banned during the Fascist regime: *Star Dust, Dancing Cheek to Cheek, Begin the Beguine* . . . I danced to some of them when my father decided to throw a party for the farm-hands and their friends before leaving the castle. It was a warm summer night. Food had been commandeered from the farm and the black market and the strong wine of Piemonte was on every table. We danced in the moonlight on the threshing-floor and in the courtyards which had been decorated with flowers and flags: the Italian *tricolore* alternated with red flags. Some of the men were singing patriotic songs and others played the accordion; the wine was flowing freely and everybody was in a happy mellow mood. Father opened the dance with me whirling around the floor to the notes of *Roll out the barrel* and everybody clapped their hands. Before taking me back to my seat he lifted my hand to his lips and kissed it. How grateful I was to those delightful old ladies who had put dancing on their long list of things for me to learn when we were living in the village near Monza! I felt immensely flattered that most of the young men were coming to ask my father for permission to dance with me. And they addressed me with the polite form of *lei* instead of the usual *tu* reserved for children. Amazing! And I danced and drank and laughed well into the night; in a way it was my coming out party!

A week after the party, my father was asked to go and manage a Home for partisans somewhere on the west coast and mother and I left for Milan. The countryside presented a most beautiful spectacle of fresh vegetation when I last looked at it as we drove away, one morning in that late spring of 1945, myriads of wild flowers everywhere and the castle surrounded by a multitude of rose bushes which seemed to have all suddenly burst into blossom. Were I to paint my memories of that period of my life, I would sketch a castle with climbing roses on its walls, a moat around it and, in a corner, a small black figure of a seminarist.

Our train was late in coming. It was a very long one and when it finally reached our station it was already full to capacity. It was bursting with people, some of them holding themselves precariously on the steps of the carriages, their clothes flying in the wind, others sticking their heads out of the window in search of some air. Scrambling to get in, the crowd on the platform pushed them back into the already full compartments. Mother and I managed to squeeze ourselves in with them and we were amazed to see the amount of luggage, parcels and bundles piled up in the racks or left around the passage. It was a long journey, the train was travelling very slowly as if the weight of all of us was too much for it. Now and then it would stop for long pauses in the middle of the countryside but, nearing Milan, we began to see traces of bombardment and destruction. We arrived, hungry and exhausted, when it was already dark and walking down the gangway we were once more surrounded, pushed and pulled by a tremendous press of people who had come to town with the impossible task of finding a roof over their heads.

As thousands of others had the same idea, the town was swamped by people looking around for accommodation. Some trying to return to their homes, often found huge holes where their houses had been. *I senza tetto* (the homeless) we were called; a terse description. Eventually we found rooms in a small hotel and, later on, we could go and share a flat with some friends in what had been a charming little street in the heart of the town, but at that time the building in which we went to live was the only one left standing in the middle of a large area covered with rubble.

Everything was difficult or impossible to find, from food to soap to petrol, and the long queues outside the shops were often formed by grumbling and disgruntled citizens. I couldn't help admiring mother who was already nearing sixty but had stood up to those recent trials with a great deal of good will and stamina. The war was over but the country was in a terrible shape and utterly broken-down. The few industries which had escaped destruction hadn't yet begun to function and the real recovery would come later with America's Marshall plan but, in the meantime, unemployment was going to increase and people would continue to buy the few things available with ration cards.

The day after our arrival at the hotel in Milan we heard that Mussolini, who had tried to flee the country with his mistress, had been captured near the Swiss border and taken prisoner by some partisans who had shot them both.

Now the whole town was in turmoil. "They have brought Mussolini to Milan," "He is at Piazzale Loreto!" "Mussolini and his gang are here!" people were shouting at each other. I had gone out to buy some soap and a tooth-brush and on my way back to the hotel I met Giorgio who short of breath, was running in the opposite direction. Giorgio was one of Michele's comrades whom I had met in Monza. "Come along," he said, barely stopping, "Come on to Piazzale Loreto and see what they have done to him. You must come, everybody should see him now." I followed him. "What are you all doing now? How is Michele?" I tried to ask him as we were running towards the square. "Well, well," he replied "We are all well." But he was hardly listening. He took hold of my hand and kept repeating excitedly, "Hurry, hurry, can't you run faster?".

As we were nearing the square we found ourselves in the middle of a crowd and, unable to make our way through it, we were pushed slowly forward towards its centre. People were coming into the square from all sides and their faces reflected the various feelings which moved them; there was awe, disgust, revenge and even triumph on those faces but also pity for the man who had been responsible for so much of their own suffering but who was now dead in front of them. Some had come with their families and the children kept close to their parents. A few women were crying softly; we pushed and elbowed our way through them. There was a strange silence all around us. In the middle of Piazzale Loreto there was a raised scaffolding. On it, hanging upside down with their feet tied to a hangman's rope, were the bodies of Mussolini, his mistress and a few others. It was a horrible sight. The dead bodies had been carried all the way from Dongo, on lake Como, where they had been shot, to the square in Milan and hung there for all the world to see! I was staring in horror at them. How long had they been dead? A day, a week perhaps, I felt weak in my knees. People around me were taking snapshots. I had lost sight of Giorgio. An elderly man who was standing next to me, said not unkindly, "Go away, go home, little girl, this is no place for you." I pushed my way out of the crowd and fled, tears running down my cheeks.

This was the first impact that post-war Milan had on me and it was ghastly. Nor was it going to improve with time. Looking back on those years immediately after the war, I see them mostly dark and unhappy with penury, misery and hurt pride. Even now after so many years, I find it extremely painful to talk about them. Some memories I have forcefully erased from my recollection but there are some events which I cannot help remembering as they are still so vividly engraved on my mind.

I remember answering the telephone one afternoon and being told that daddy had suffered a heart attack and had been rushed to hospital. I felt as if my own heart had been damaged, it beat so loudly whilst I jotted down the name and address of the hospital that I felt it was going to burst. He had been taken ill in his office at the Home for partisans while he was attending a meeting, and a doctor had been immediately called for. Mother and I put a few things in a suitcase and got on the first train to Genoa. There we had a long wait before catching another train to Ventimiglia and by the time we reached our destination it was quite late at night. When we finally got to the hospital we found him in the intensive care ward where he was going to stay for the next three weeks. We found rooms nearby and spent our days at his bedside. When he eventually got better and was allowed to go home, mother nursed him tirelessly and lovingly. She had been a Red Cross nurse during the Great War and was very capable and efficient.

Daddy recovered in time but was too weak to resume his work at the Home for partisans. Later he tried to find another job. He went about looking for work, couldn't find any, and day after day he came back empty-handed, feeling even more depressed and useless to himself and his family. Bit by bit he sold the last pieces of jewellery we had. He talked very little during that last period of his life and lost a great amount of weight. *E' arrivata Clementina, sorriso della vita* (Here is Clementina, the smile of our lives) he had written many years before under one of my first photographs, and indeed I was the only one who could cheer him up. But I was very anxious for him and so painfully aware of my parents' precarious financial condition that I found it difficult to make myself smile. I remember writing out little cards with the word "smile" in capital letters and leaving them about in the bathroom and on my dressing-table in order to remind myself continuously of the necessity to look cheerful for my parents' sake. But I wasn't very good at it and still played at being a grown-up. I was nearing the end of my school life, and I hadn't as yet any clear idea of what I would be doing with my life. My father, who had only the prospect of an uncertain and possibly painful future in front of him, wanted me to go on to university in spite of his financial difficulties. But in his usual unpractical way, he wanted me to read humanities because he believed, poor dear, that I had a good brain and that I should continue my classical education.

Mother, on the other hand, wasn't so keen on the idea and suggested that I should do a secretarial course immediately after graduation. So what should I do? I was uncertain and undecided, there were so many things that I wanted to do but none especially. In one of my letters to Laura I asked for her advice. She was still in Monza but was hoping to come to Milan the following year to enrol at the University of Medicine. She took up her role of adviser very actively and suggested in her neatly written letters that I should seriously consider becoming a doctor like her. "Think!" she would write affectionately, "We could work together and, perhaps, even share a flat." That would have been the maximum of independence for a girl of my background and I could hardly believe it possible, but her enthusiasm was contagious and I more or less convinced myself that that was what I really wanted to do. The idea appealed to me. Even in real life, and not only in my make-believe world, I wished to be of some help to my fellow human beings and what would be better than to cure their many ills?

In the meantime I was attending my last year at high school. Although my formal education was nearing its end there was still a world of things which I didn't know and of which I didn't even suspect the existence. All sorts of things connected with sex, for instance, were still a mystery to me. Mother, of course, would never dream of enlightening me. "You'll find out when you get married," she would repeat the few times that I dared put some question to her.

She was still very strict and I had to account for every hour of my day and for every person that I saw. All make-up had been so far forbidden to me. To put some colour on my lips I used to rub them against the edge of my exercise-books which were badly dyed a bright red and I had to remember to wash it off before going home. One day I decided to be bold and challenge this ban on cosmetics. With the help of an obliging school-friend who carried a vanity case in her bag, I busied myself in the dark cloakroom of the school, putting real lipstick on my lips, plenty of rouge on my cheeks and powder on my shiny nose. Having completed my new face by using a black crayon on my eyebrows, I combed my hair with a parting on one side and I let it fall on my face in the style of Veronica Lake which I believed was the height of glamour. Looking at myself in the mirror I thought that I looked simply smashing, not realising that having made up my face under the electric light, I had overdone it quite considerably. I walked out into the daylight expecting everybody in the street to look at me in stark admiration and, in fact, a boy or two turned their heads in my direction and another whistled his appreciation. I was on my way to a girl-friend's house where I was to spend the afternoon studying and by the time I had left her to go home for dinner, I had completely forgotten about the make-up.

"Clementina! What have you done to your face?" my mother exclaimed in a horrified tone as soon as I came in. "You have been putting make-up on," she added accusingly, pointing her finger at my lips. "Shame on you! Wait until I've told your father about it." Father wasn't pleased either. "This is ridiculous!" he said as soon as he saw me, "You look just like a tart, go and wash your face immediately." I retreated in confusion, my face red as a tomato, and I did as I was told. But what was really ridiculous I came to realise later, was that at the age of seventeen, I didn't really know what a tart did do although it was clear that she was doing something bad with men and that it was shameful to be one and practically equally so to look like one. "I'll find out one day," I said hopefully to myself as I dried my face with a towel.

But I had little time for pursuing this or any other line of enquiry because the rest of that period was taken up with the preparation for my finals. It had also become clear that I would do well to follow my mother's advice and sensibly begin to look for a job as soon as possible.

Saying goodbye to my idea of becoming a doctor, I started privately a course of typing and shorthand. My teacher was an elderly woman, enormously fat and extraordinarily bad-tempered. She lived by herself in a dingy flat on the outskirts of the town. It took me almost two hours to get to her, changing two trams and walking down a depressing alley flanked by decrepit and ugly houses; almost a slum. Her flat consisted of two rooms and a kitchenette where the dust had long ago taken possession of the scanty furniture, slowly turning into soot. Near the kitchen window, on a small round table there was a cage with a canary in it. An old bottle of milk, a few half-empty jars and some stale bread littered the shelves near the gas stove. There was always a faint smell of stale food lingering around the place. Mrs Brambilla, as she was called, was a widow. Her husband had died back in 1939, the concierge of the building had once explained, when she had stopped me to ask where I was going. "Ah, la Signora Brambilla . . . that one," she had said, "You would be too young to remember but her story had made the front pages of the newspapers. A scandal . . . a thing like that happening during the Fascist era. You can't imagine . . . a real scandal it was! Poor Signora Brambilla."

Having thus wetted my interest, I begged her to continue with her story. Apparently Signor Brambilla had left her a few years previous to his death having declared to all and sundry that she was too ugly, too fat and too bad-tempered for anyone in his right senses to go on living with her. He had consequently disappeared from the neighbourhood leaving behind a great quantity of debts which his wife had eventually paid, out of her meagre typist's pay. Signor Brambilla had gone to live the life of a tramp in a hut out in the fields which surrounded the southern part of Milan, presumably enjoying his new-found freedom. One day he had been found dead by one of his chums who, not having seen him for a while, had gone to his hut to find out what had become of him. He had discovered his two-week-old body half eaten by rats. Somehow, this discovery had reached the papers and, as it was unthinkable that things like this could happen in the healthy, clean and well-organised society of the Fascist era, it became a sort of political scandal in which it was implied that this degenerated man (tramps officially didn't exist any more) had been a communist bent on subversive actions. Mrs Brambilla, his legal if unwanted wife, had to suffer the brunt of her connection with him and had to leave her job. She had since managed to make ends meet by giving typing lessons.

When I first met her she was still definitely not a pretty sight, what with being so much overweight and having all those warts and bumps on her face and bent legs which made it so difficult for her to negotiate the flights of stairs leading to her sixth-floor flat. In fact, not having a telephone or a lift, she often waited for me to arrive at her doorstep before asking me to go down again and do some shopping for her: "Young people have good legs," she would say on such occasions with a finality difficult to contradict, "So I'm sure you don't mind running down the steps for me."

She had quarrelled with her next-door neighbours and she must have felt quite lonely and helpless at times. I never met anyone at her place. The scruffy building in which she had her flat, was mainly occupied by noisy and violent people and often climbing up the many stairs to go to my lesson, I could hear shouts and swear words coming from their flats.

My poor teacher was often seized by fits of terrible coughing which made her gasp for air and turn alarmingly purple in the face. On such occasions she would stop her teaching and send me home. Because of all these things she charged very little for her lessons.

Although she could be very choleric during her lessons and would shout at me in such a way that I almost sympathised with the late Mr Brambilla, she must have hidden a good heart behind her irascible façade because sometimes she volunteered to make me a well-known home-made tonic, the *zabaglione*. It was made with the yoke of an egg beaten with sugar and Marsala wine in which crushed eggshells had infused for months supposedly to provide calcium to fortify the debilitated. "Drink it, drink it down," she would tell me looking at me critically with her sharp little eyes. "You look so thin, how you expect to find a job and hold it, I can't imagine!" And she would make me drink her concoction. It was very strong, and often the wine would go to my head.

I never learnt how to type properly. I found her lessons extremely boring especially after having so often vividly imagined my first year of anatomy in the most gruesome and excitingly bloody terms. However, I eventually managed to get a diploma in shorthand and typing and set out to look for a job. I got one almost at once with a chemical company; its factory was situated on the outskirts of the town and to be there at eight o'clock I had to get up at a quarter-to-six. Instead of doing secretarial work I was told to do some laboratory work which consisted literally in messing about with colours. In fact, what with the fumes of the chemicals and the acids and the long hours, I soon became ill and my hair turned to an incredible green tinge. As I hated the job it was almost a relief to have to resign on doctor's advice and once more look around for a better position. Through the help of one of my father's influential friends, I was soon engaged as a secretary to a young executive of a large industrial concern with headquarters in Milan. I shared with another girl a most luxurious office which was near those of our two bosses. She was a very experienced and efficient girl who dealt with her work calmly and professionally. I was a disaster! An utterly useless secretary, what with my general incompetence, bad typing and excessive shyness. I was so self-conscious that I would misdial a number only because somebody was watching me using the telephone and that somebody was generally my own boss! I would make all the mistakes possible at my disposal as a secretary to a fast-rising, ambitious man.

Sheets of paper were generally held together with pins instead of clips. Right-handed people put the pin through the sheets in the top left corner with the head of the pin *up*. But, being left-handed and so often absent-minded, I would insert the pin with the head *down* causing the sharp end of it to prick my boss's fingers and sometimes draw blood!

I seem to have suffered from dyslexia during office hours. My nervous fingers at the typewriter keyboard would spell *daer* instead of dear and *sinrecely yuors* without my even noticing the mistake. And when I did notice I would hand him my freshly-typed sheets often defaced with small holes where I had rubbed away a spelling mistake with too much energy.

Because of the speed necessary to process the vast quantities of documentation which found their way to my filing cabinet, I often filed things out of date order with the obvious result that it took me a long time to trace a paper when I needed it most. Sometimes my boss would help me by searching for it himself, especially when he wanted it in a hurry and the occasional visitor would find us buried in files which were scattered all over the desk, and often on the floor, while my poor boss would mutter, "Chaos, chaos everywhere." When the long-suffering man could take no more, he would go to the window, lift his hands above his head and say in wonder, "Signorina, lei é al di là di ogni immaginazione!" (You are beyond any imagination).

But he was a kind and obviously patient man who kept my job open to me even when I had to leave it for six months. I was often absent from work because I suffered from an endless stream of illnesses culminating in typhoid fever. Most probably he was glad of the chance I gave him to get some work properly done by one of the girls from the typist pool who would substitute for me!

My parents had moved once more to the countryside and I was living in Milan in the flat of some people who seldom used it and, therefore, let it to me for a small rent. I remember how tickled and gratified I was when I received my first salary in a neat envelope at the end of my first working month. Of course, paying out the rent of the flat was another source of satisfaction, like working out my budget, adding up figures and generally administering my life. That was it! Now obviously I was really grown-up—I knew no one of my own age who was in the same position as myself; living alone was going to be an intoxicating experience. Laura, who had finally come to Milan to study medicine, was living at a youth hostel and the other young people I had recently met were all still living with their parents.

In fact, it was an intoxicating experience during the day (I had even told people in the office that I lived quite alone in the flat, arousing some admiration and a little envy among the other girls) but at night, moving through the empty flat I was more than a little scared. Still, this was freedom I reassured myself, freedom to do what I wanted, to come and go, to eat and sleep whenever I felt like it. No more supervision, no more restrictions or strict punctuality. Marvellous! Of course, it was a great pity that my new-found freedom was severely taxed by having to keep office hours and by the fact that I didn't quite know what to do with it nor, for a long time to come, would I take advantage of it, but still, it was a beginning.

My bedroom was very comfortable and cheerful. It was a wide room with a high ceiling and its window faced south so that it was warm and sunny. It had a large Victorian wooden bed with a pretty bedcover made of a chintzy material which matched the curtains. The furniture was also old, a walnut wardrobe stood in one corner, and a desk with a chair with a velvet seat in the other. A kidney-shaped dressing-table covered with glass to protect it from the smears of make-up, stood in front of the window and the inlaid chest-of-drawers was put opposite the bed.

From my third floor balcony I looked over the horse-chestnuts in the street below and, in the distance, I could see the Castello Sforzesco and the tips of the trees which surrounded it. Another great advantage was that the flat was near my office which I could reach by tram in about ten minutes.

I came home for lunch every day. It generally varied from capuccino with a pair of croissants to some chestnut purée which I ate directly from the jar using a spoon while, stretched out on my bed, I would read a book or listen to some records. When they were in season, I would gorge myself with strawberries, cherries and figs which were cheap and plentiful. Bread and butter was really my staple diet as I never cooked anything at home. Considering this diet, it was not surprising that I often suffered from tummy-ache. Fortunately the owners of the flat, an elderly couple without children, came to Milan once or twice a week taking their maid with them and we would eat together some sensible food which kept me going till the next time.

I spent Sundays with my parents in the country. During the first months I hardly saw anyone but Laura whom I met after office hours. She had been disappointed that her idea of sharing a flat with me had been turned down by our parents as being too forward. We were genuinely fond of each other; a strange thing, in a way, as we were also very different in looks and temperament. I admired her greatly but I couldn't really see what she saw in me. As I have already mentioned, she was most stunning in what abroad is considered a typical Italian beauty. She was very sure of herself, a calm and responsible girl without the uncertainties and doubts which troubled me. She never seemed to have had any problems in growing up, she had always been mature and reliable. Perhaps, she felt attracted to me just because of this seriousness of hers which prevented her from enjoying the silliness typical of our young age. I had plenty of it on the other hand, I was romantic, sentimental, emotional and passionate (although I didn't realise it then), often swinging from tears to laughter and, most of all, immensely curious.

I wanted to see everything, do everything and try everything . . . in theory. In practice the many taboos and restraints imposed on me by my mother and more still by my background, would have made it next to impossible for me to take advantage of a total freedom. I would have been scared stiff of it.

But Laura, on the contrary, having already made most of her choices, led her organised and constructive life without self-doubts or second thoughts. She would soon make a circle of friends who had the same outlook as herself. Still, she hung on to me and hardly a day passed without a telephone call from her. She used to say jokingly that I was her only idiosyncrasy in her well-regulated life.

Later on, when she decided to get married, she chose a quiet and intelligent young doctor, just as serious as she was and with the same interests as herself, with whom she could share a pleasant life without the complications and tortures of a passionate love affair. I don't think she was ever in love, she just cared, deeply but reasonably for her man from whom, in time, she had two children.

Laura went about looking for a suitable man in her usual down to earth way. At the time of her courtship with Maurizio (that was the name of her beau) she told me, one day, that she had decided that it would be sensible to go to bed with him before actually marrying him just in case "things were not so good in that respect", as she put it to me. "How can you do such a thing in cold blood?" I remonstrated deeply shocked;" This is the sure way to make him leave you afterwards!" I went on, trying to make her desist from her purpose, with little hope of succeeding. As a matter of fact, "everything went off satisfactorily", to use once more her own words and a year later they were married. And as far as one can see they have been happy ever since. So she had been right, but like most of the young people I had recently met, I was still too immature to know about such things and too frightened of sex. It took us all a long time to see through the barriers of prejudice and the strict upbringing.

When my parents were still living in Milan they had renewed their friendship with a number of their old friends and distant relations and through them I had come to know these young people with whom I kept in touch. They all belonged to what was then called by people who didn't belong to it, sarcastically and perhaps a little enviously, *la jeunesse dorée,* and despite my frequent unwell periods, despite having to be very careful with my money if I wanted to buy myself some decent clothes to go out with them, I managed to lead quite a busy, gay, social life. I shall try to describe it presently.

On the other hand Laura had introduced me to some of her student-friends who were mostly middle-class intellectuals of the left and with whom I occasionally shared a plate of spaghetti and a glass of wine.

But, on the whole, I saw little of them, partly because Laura, being so single-minded in her studies, considered a waste of time any form of social gathering and partly because I felt slightly ill at ease with them. My colossal prudery made me shudder in embarrassment at their easy and promiscuous ways. Not that my virginity was ever in danger, nobody took me seriously there as I was still that *ragazzina,* Laura's little friend; and I behaved like one, I hate to say. Being told casually that the two young men I had recently met were gay, I looked upon them as if they were some devilish personages out of the *mala vita* the underworld, used as I was to good society where situations like that were completely ignored. It is interesting to notice in passing that in the rare cases in which such men were mentioned, one would use a quaint expression to describe them: "They belonged," one said, "to the other parish church!"

However, those students were mostly impatient young men, brilliantly and angrily seeking knowledge and self-expression, and already slightly frustrated in their hopes for a just socialistic society. Just the opposite of my sedate young friends whose lives had been safely shaped by their parents who, in spite of the great changes the war had brought along in the wake of its destruction and violence, had retained a profound conservative outlook on life.

Those were important years for us who were young after the war. We were all busy young people, some of us very active in social work and all looking at the future with optimism and new hopes. Everything had to be rebuilt, redone and rethought after the devastation of the war and twenty years of Fascist rule. It was an exciting time and we all wanted to contribute and do our bit in helping our country to become once again a democracy with a new social order.

We went to concerts, plays and lectures. Some of my young friends were still attending university and their parents would often provide the tickets; otherwise we would get standing only, and for the first time in our lives we would listen to Beethoven perhaps played by Backhaus, or Chopin by Benedetti-Michelangeli and applaud Toscanini and De Sabata. We hardly missed a concert with music by Bach or Mozart and had endless discussions about modern painters and composers. We went assiduously to La Scala which had recently been rebuilt after being bombed during the war.

My musical education having been so far, scrappy and fragmentary, I now set about to widen it. I plunged into this pleasant task with my usual enthusiasm. Borrowing an old gramophone and a great quantity of records, I listened to them with great concentration, playing the same piece over and over again. But not having a good ear was frustrating to the extreme, I could never pick up a tune on the key-board or sing aloud long enough without being asked, in no uncertain way, to shut up. So although I got a great deal out of it, I had to content myself with a superficial knowledge of the classical work and turn my attention to books.

We read furiously all the Russian, French and American authors as well as our Italian ones to the extent that eventually some of us acquired an intellectual bent while others became bent intellectuals!

Laura and I started reading books on psychology and eastern philosophy which opened up new dimensions in my life. I understood better the problems which had attracted us when we were still at school and while for Laura reading philosophy was mainly an intellectual exercise, I found it extremely reassuring to discover that the world of the grown-ups had many facets, that there were many sides to one question, that there were other people like me who, unable to accept the dogmatism of the Catholic thinking, had turned to other possibilities and other choices; I was no longer alone in my doubts. I felt deeply attracted to Buddhism, for me an, utterly new way of looking at life and death and it influenced my way of thinking in years to come. But, most of all and I might mention this just in passing, as the years went by, I learned the importance of having courage in life: courage to live, to be oneself, courage to overcome difficulties and sorrows. I also learned to appreciate solitude and kindness. Perhaps kindness most of all. I remember being immensely impressed by what Aldous Huxley had to say during a conference at an American university, if I'm not mistaken, not long before he died: "It is a little embarrasing," he said, "that, after forty-five years of research and study, the best advice I can give to people is to be a little kinder to each other."

Whenever we could take advantage of a few days off we went sight-seeing. Europeans in general, and we Italians in particular, are very fortunate in living as we do surrounded by marvellous works of art. We absorb beauty in a natural way whilst walking in our streets, praying in our churches, driving around the countryside and visiting museums. This is especially so in Italy where every village, even the smallest hamlet, has its own masterpiece.

One of the most unforgettable memories of my life will always be the first time I saw Venice. It took my breath away. Like everybody else I had seen pictures and documentaries of the city but nothing can adequately recreate the atmosphere of the place. It was sheer delight to splash about San Marco Square which was flooded for a few hours, to sit in a gondola in the Canal Grande, to walk its *calli,* to visit its churches. Like any tourists we fed its pigeons, we admired its glasses and we walked everywhere, trying to take in this unique and unequalled jewel of a city; to me Venice will always be the most charming proof of the genius of the Italians.

Another time Laura and I travelled south. That required a little more organisation because we were going to be away almost a week. In fact, what was meant to be just a few days trip turned out, even before we set foot on the train, into a major operation. It would have been the first time the two of us would have faced the dangers of a journey alone and, not surprisingly, our parents put the veto on the idea. We would be allowed to go but only in the company of a suitable adult. For some reason the search for this *persona appropriata* was full of difficulties and when, at last, we found one in Laura's great aunt, everybody was dissatisfied with the choice: Laura didn't like her, I thought she was too old to stand the journey and the aunt herself didn't really want to travel!

Auntie and her luggage

We took off one Saturday, after office hours, to find out that *la zietta* (auntie) had taken enough luggage with her to last for a few months. Although it was the end of June, she explained that she was afraid to catch cold and during the length of the journey she spent her time putting on and taking off a great quantity of garments which were supposed to protect her from the evil effects of a draught, from excess of perspiration or from the humidity of the night. That meant that we were obliged to carry for her half-a-dozen garments on top of a rather heavy handbag in which she kept a vast quantity of medicines. She complained all the way about one thing and another and she made it quite clear from the start that she had only come as a favour to Laura's father. She was a great pain in the neck. However, Laura and I were in high spirits and managed to enjoy our trip in spite of her.

We got off the train at Naples but we avoided visiting it too thoroughly because it was still in the grip of the most tragic shambles in the aftermath of the war years and we headed for Pompeii, Paestum and Capri. Laura, more than I, was a conscientious tourist determined not to miss anything and at times the going was exhausting even for me. Auntie would give up almost at once and would sit fanning herself with a handkerchief on a chair in a café, creating logistic problems for us. For me the true south begins on reaching the environs of Naples and one could see the effects of a torrid climate on the parched earth; it was stifling. At Pompeii the sun was beating down with such intensity that I couldn't remember ever having felt so hot during my years in Libya. Africa begins at Rome northern Italians often like to say with more irony than truth but, at the time, I was almost inclined to agree with them! When the *scirocco*—the hot and humid south wind—came up we were soon all covered with a thin, whitish dust which forced auntie to wear a large white scarf over her head and shoulders giving her a ghost-like appearance!

We sought the help of a guide, an elderly man with a thick Neapolitan accent which we found hard to understand. He showed us around but as I discovered later, he also managed to avoid showing us the most erotic frescoes and the most revealing statues. The old Romans of my history books came alive once more in that incredible town, half preserved by the lava of Vesuvius, where one could still see their houses, their villas, shops and streets. Pompeii reminded me of a Sleeping Beauty. At any moment I expected to see its people suddenly come out of their houses and gather noisily in the squares or go about their business in their shops as they had so long ago.

I remember going across the Bay of Naples on a ferry-boat to Capri under the most torrential rain. The sea was rough and Laura's aunt was miserably seasick. She called upon all the saints in heaven to take her out of her misery and swore that, never again would she accompany us anywhere; we were pitiless, selfish girls who had no consideration for the elderly. She had a point there, as we had been rushing for the last three days at a punishing pace following Laura's inexorable drive. Capri was the last stage of our trip. "You'll be my death," the poor thing kept repeating "Santa Maria, what have I done to deserve this?" But Laura was unrepentant and dragged us around the enchanting island.

Luckily the sun had come out and we were able to enjoy the most superb view of the Faraglioni and to visit Axel Munthe's villa at Anacapri. Travelling all night by train, I managed to be in my office the next morning with one more reason to be a useless secretary—I could hardly keep my eyes open!

This was also the last trip Laura and I did together because she was soon to become engaged to Maurizio and also because her aunt refused, with some reason, to have anything to do with us again!

When my next two weeks holiday came by, I was asked by a girlfriend, Giulia, to stay in her parents' villa in the lovely countryside north of Milan. Those houses, scattered all around that part of Lombardy, had a particular charm of their own. Often very large and surrounded by a huge park, they were generally used during the summer and early autumn months. Now they were full of young people ready to enjoy themselves. I had always considered myself privileged to have been able to share with them in so much beauty, gracious living and cultured background in spite of my almost Cinderella-like status. If, at times, it was inevitable that I experienced pangs of hurt pride, on the other hand I felt adult and responsible for being the only girl within the group who was supporting herself.

Giulia, a lovely red-haired girl with a tall slim figure, was becoming a good friend of mine. If she didn't inspire in me the great affection which I felt for Laura, on the other hand she made me share her tremendous sense of fun and bubbling lightness of touch. I could be silly with her, a luxury that Laura would never have allowed!

We belonged to the youngest group—between the ages of seventeen and twenty-one—and we cycled all around the countryside visiting each other; we played tennis and held dancing parties in the afternoons. We kept a journal and, now and then, someone would write a portrait or paint one. As one would expect, the written portraits were all in a highly poetic, literary style, extremely flourishing and romantic, typical of the students' rather precocious esoteric way of expressing themselves; here is one about me written by a girlfriend which freely translated, sounded more or less like this:

Clementina

Clementina, pale and blonde, pale like the shadow of a white camellia, her eyes a shade darker than the gold of her hair; her amber eyes seem to question from within the depth of tragedy.

Her soft face is vaguely reminiscent of something seen elsewhere, perhaps a Van Dyck portrait, where a princess in a large plumed hat absent-mindedly strokes a reclining greyhound.

Or perhaps she is just a vision in the moonlight, dancing so lightly that her feet seem not to touch the ground, a passing image with the keen nostalgia of her race in her troubled smile. Perhaps past memories, as if her slender shoulders were already burdened with an evanescent past.

Vividly surrounded by candlelight, clothed in fine lace and vermillion, her small feet in a pair of embroidered red slippers, she listens to a polonaise, her eyes flashing under the aureole of her shimmering golden hair.

Or languid in a white cloud of muslim, a lingering perfume of gardenias in the air, she walks demurely among cypress trees, her lips as red as the rose she holds in her white hand.

But perhaps what we love most about her is to sense her unawareness of all the things we see in her when she appears, fair and ethereal, amongst her friends!

Practically during the whole period of my stay, there were picnics, tea-parties and games. A very popular one was the game of truth in which by answering truthfully to a set of questions we would indicate, among giggles and blushes, our preference for a boy or a girl in our group.

We were never expected to do any housework or cooking but we were encouraged to make our beds and arrange the flowers which the gardener would take to the pantry every morning.

It was there that for the first time I had a vague notion of what flirting was all about. Chaste as our dancing was, I sometimes felt a funny sensation in my stomach when my partner held me in his arms and against his chest. This strange sensation made me feel self-conscious to the point of making me dance stiffly, whilst a false sense of decency prevented me from discussing it with the other girls. It is almost impossible now to believe how innocent and naive we were and how seriously we took ourselves!

We were so well brought up, so well-mannered, so refined; most of the girls were still chaperoned. We were expected to behave in a ladylike way (which comprised quite a long list of do's and an even longer one of don'ts), to be reasonably beautiful and to find a suitable husband as soon as expedient. He should be possibly handsome, preferably a member of the aristocracy and undoubtedly rich. Sex was a total taboo, we talked little about it and practised even less. We discovered that the few old women who vaguely talked to us about it belonged to different schools of thought. Giulia's grandmother (who was the mother of six children) once tried to put us in the picture explaining that physical love was very important to men but that most women didn't care for it; nevertheless they should submit to their husband's requests. To divert herself from the whole distasteful business a wife could make up a shopping list in her mind of all the things she would need next day! The other school touched the miraculous: somehow during the ceremony of holy matrimony those couples who had made a suitable arranged marriage would fall in love with each other, thereafter enjoying the physical bliss of married life!

Most of us were very romantic. I remember going to see that popular film *The Lady of the Camellias* in which the heroine is dying of love and consumption, and using three borrowed handkerchiefs to soak up my tears. Also Giulia, who didn't wash her right hand for three whole days because her beau had kissed it; I can still see her taking a bath with her hand up above her head! And our crush on Leslie Howard in *Gone with the Wind* and our dislike for Clark Gable whom we considered not sophisticated enough for our tastes!

Dancing cheek to cheek was considered fast and if a boy was so carried away as to kiss a girl on the mouth he would probably do so with his lips closed; it would have been a tremendous lack of respect to do it any other way! Girls in general were divided into two categories: *them* and *us*. *Them* were the women of easy virtue, shop-girls or downright whores whom the boys often visited because a young man must have his experience and because a hot-blooded male was supposed to need to satisfy his sexual urges (Giulia claimed that her brothers couldn't keep away from them for longer than a day or two), but of course, when the time came they were expected to marry a young woman of their own class.

But *them* were also those girls not quite so nice, who went in for some petting. Once identified by our parents they were gently but firmly eased out of our group as unsuitable and slightly dangerous company who might lead us astray. We didn't mind seeing them go because they generally looked down on us as greenhorns even refusing to discuss their promiscuous life with us. Most of all, we were glad to see the back of them because we had noticed that our boys would make a bee-line for them whenever they were around.

"Young ladies should take great care to remain so," the nuns had often warned us, adding that any form of petting was bad for our health. It was thought to cause acne and palpitations.

We heard more about the advantages of keeping our total innocence when Giulia and I joined a small group of girls who, safely escorted by two nuns and enlightened by a guide, went down to Rome for a three-day visit to the Vatican Museums and St. Peter's Cathedral.

We stayed at a hostel which was very near the Borghese Museum but a stop there was frowned upon by the nuns on account of Canova's famous statue of Paolina Borghese, Napoleon's sister, reclining on a couch only partially covered by a thin veil. Most unsuitable—they said—and we were taken directly to St. Peter's where our eloquent guide lost no time in instructing us in an admirable and learned way. But when we stopped in front of Michelangelo's *Pietă*, portraying the Holy Virgin holding the body of Christ in her arms, our guide remarked "The Holy Virgin looks so young despite the fact that she was the mother of a thirty-three year old son, because virginity keeps one young! Ah, young ladies," he said, "Don't you ever forget it: la verginità mantiene giovani."

During the winter months, especially at carnival, my friends held many parties in their old palaces full of wonderful old furniture, priceless paintings and "works of art". These parties were formal gatherings with the girls in long dresses and the boys in dark suits and ties. Sometimes as we arrived, very punctually, we would be greeted by the parents who would stay on with us until the very end. They would sit with a couple of friends in a corner of the drawing-room or ballroom, inspecting and discussing the young guests among themselves; how their presence irritated us! We would dance until very late or rather till the early hours of the morning and sometimes go from there on to a nearby church to hear mass, still in our evening clothes. There was a lot of laughter and romance at those parties and, tremendously appreciated, lots of food, a great variety of it, which was laid out on the dining-table on silver plates. After the lean years of the war it was really a delicious sight for all of us and for me especially; not having eaten anything the whole day, I was almost faint with hunger!

Eventually some of the young men proposed to me. I remember my great excitement when one of them began courting me. That took the form of escorting me home last so that we could be alone for a little while and sitting next to me at the cinema trying to touch my arm with his elbow as he would have never dared to hold my hand. He would dance with me as many dances as he could manage, before some other boys beat him to it, impatiently waiting each time for the next record to be put on. He asked me to dance only with him the song *You Belong to my Heart*, perhaps hoping that I would either understand the meaning of the English words (which I didn't) or have them translated for me (which I did). Once he got so carried away by his feelings that he kissed me on the mouth, lips firmly closed, and, fired by his own daring, he proposed to me. We would get married when he finished university and when he was sure to be able to support me in the

style to which he was accustomed! How long would that take? He
couldn't tell, but he thought it would take quite a while and, in the
meantime, we would keep it as a secret between us. It was such a
well-kept secret that, after a while, somebody else proposed to
me. This one came from South America, a young man of Italian
origin, whose father had sent back to Italy to find an Italian
wife for himself. She needn't be rich as his family was quite well
off, but she had to come from a good family. I was the obvious
choice as not many of the other girls were prepared to follow him
to the other side of the world. I believe that what upset him most
about my refusal to marry him was the thought of going back to his
father empty-handed! After all, he had been given six months to
come, see and conquer!

Another self-assured young man whom I met on the French
Riviera, where I stayed with some friends during my next leave,
was a Swiss, Fritz. He intensely disliked, and made fun of, things
Italian and nothing, but nothing, that we Italians had done or
presumably would do in the future would meet with his approval.
And now he found himself in love with an Italian girl! What a
drama! But his feelings for me were so strong as to make him
overlook his prejudices and he set about offering me the best of all
possible worlds. He used to tell me with great insistence and in all
seriousness that he belonged to one of the best families of the best
town in the best canton of the best country on earth. How could
one refuse the chance to belong to such a set-up?

I had gone to the Riviera during the second part of August to
stay with some hospitable new friends I had met at various parties
during the last carnival season in Milan. They were the classical
nouveaux riches and they splashed their money about in a way that
slightly alarmed and embarrassed me. They had the latest sports
cars, the fastest boats and a swimming-pool in the garden of their
villa above Cap Ferrat which was furnished with all kinds of garish
and showy luxuries. They were a family of four, the father,
Commendatore Pirola who, it was whispered, had made most of
his money in the black market during the war, was a jolly fellow
with drive and good nature but a slightly common appearance. He
sported a diamond ring on his hairy finger and his hair shone with
brilliantine. His wife was a plump little woman with dyed blonde
hair, a lot of make-up on her sun-tanned face and rows of golden

chains around her double chin. She was fond of pointing out that she came from a better background than her husband, the Commendatore, something that otherwise would have passed completely unnoticed.

She complained endlessly of *crise de foie*. The two daughters had been finished at a college in Switzerland and, like their parents, they were dying to be accepted by *la buona società* (good society). To reach this aim they had spent the previous winter giving lavish parties and patronising with generous donations various charities which were generally chaired by a member of the upper classes.

Having given this accurate but somewhat catty description of the people who had kindly invited me to spend some time in their midst, I must add that, having got used to their hearty and exuberant ways, I found them extremely *simpatici*. I enjoyed their generous hospitality at their Hollywood-style villa in the splendid setting of the French Riviera with grateful abandon.

After a few days of pastoral life I was asked to escort the younger daughter to Paris for a short trip. All expenses would be paid by her parents. We took off from Nice and made the trip in the style of the filthy rich (what else?), staying in an hotel off Place de la Concorde and being escorted around by an employee of her father in a chauffeur-driven limousine. We visited the most famous fashion houses, we dined at Maxim's and I wore one of her furcoats—leopard skin—and walked about the place pretending to be Gina Lollobrigida. Such luxury I had never known and for a while my socialistic soul was swept under the posh carpet of the hotel!

The last part of my holiday was spent on touring Provence. Fritz was one of the young men who would drive us around that beautiful part of France; we would make day trips and often stop at a restaurant *en route* and sample some *specialité Provençale*. Unfortunately the result of these touristic and culinary expeditions was quite dramatic; I fell ill with a very high temperature and a splitting head-ache. I came back from the sea-side with typhoid fever and the Swiss in tow!

The disease went unidentified for a long time because at first I thought that I was suffering from a bad case of flu. Having recently been away from the office for long periods suffering from a variety of minor ailments culminating in an operation to remove my appendix, I hesitated to ask once again for sick leave and I presented myself to my boss at the appointed time, ready to resume work. He welcomed me back with the hope that after so much rest and recuperation at the sea-side he would have the pleasure to see more of me from now on. "Do you feel quite well now?" he went on to enquire. "Oh, fine," I replied untruthfully, and for another week I dragged myself about feeling like death.

It was just then that the thought of death first crossed my mind. I was condemned to die, sometime certainly, like every one else and, perhaps, very soon. From the time I realised that I was mortal I found the idea unbearable and I wondered how other people managed to live their everyday lives facing this terrifying certainty. The horrible thought of my death, of my body not existing any more, filled me with such a sense of panic that finally I was ready to face my boss's eventual displeasure and called a doctor.

I was by then very sick and a priest was called to my bedside. Unconscious and therefore oblivious to what was going on around me, I remember having the most beautiful dreams. Clear psychedelic perceptions of floating between the deep blue sea, all aglitter with sun-rays, and the blue of a cloudless Mediterranean sky. *L'eternitè—c'est la mer—mêlée au soleil* wrote Rimbeau somewhere and, indeed, I felt I had reached eternity as I lay dying in bed.

I slowly recovered but later had a relapse. The only causalty was my hair which dropped out at an alarming rate and was eventually shorn off by my father one Christmas Eve.

Seeing that I was a bit downcast, daddy with his inimitable sense of the ridiculous, cheered me up by making great fun out of the situation pretending to be Figaro, the Barber of Seville; singing loud and out of tune the main arias of the opera, and mimicking with comic gestures the famous barber, he got hold of a pair of scissors and a razor and shaved off what remained of my hair.

That Christmas I received a great number of large kerchiefs and multi-coloured scarves with which I covered my bald head for the following months.

I had taken my first proposals of marriage in the most immature, superficial way without giving much thought to the boys who made them. Naturally I was very flattered by them, as they were feathers in my cap, something to boast about and discuss with my girl-friends. My heart and senses hadn't been touched as yet; I was far more involved in my own world of make-believe into which I still frequently escaped. No reality was ever as good as the stories I was making up for myself!

The man who was to change all that hadn't as yet come into my life. But it wasn't too long before I met him. When I first saw Carlo he was in his late thirties. His huge frame—he was well over six feet tall and a little stout—was dressed in casual clothes a bit old and shining with wear. His thick black hair streaked with silver, looked as if it were in permanent need of attention, his face with his dark eyes and big fleshy Arab nose and generous sensual lips was unusual in its tense and intelligent expression. He burst one day into my office looking for my boss. He had some very urgent work, would I please type it for him? He was also working for our firm but in another branch. He handed me some sheets, written in almost unreadable handwriting. I was seized by panic at the thought of having to type in front of him. But, luckily, my boss came into my office and took him out for a coffee. They didn't come back until well after my lunch break. I was still sweating and swearing in front of my typewriter battling with its keys. I handed him my badly-typed sheets, blushing with embarrassment. He put them straight into his brief-case without looking at them and thanked and complimented me for staying on. "You deserve a present" he said, "But, I'm sure that would be against company policy. Would you like to come and have lunch with me? You must be famished by now."

We went to a nearby restaurant which was full of people and smoke and where, after having been kept waiting a long time, we were given a table in the middle of the room and some very indifferent food. Carlo talked a little about his recent trip to South America but he seemed rather uninterested and absent-minded. He was also in a hurry because of a meeting he had to attend shortly and irritated because the service was very slow. So, when saying goodbye, he expressed the wish to see me soon again, I thought he was just being polite. But two days later he was back in my office, saying "Let's go and have dinner together in a little place I know. Usually the food is very good there and I want to make amends for the awful meal I gave you the other day. Will

you be free tonight? Please say yes!'' He seemed eager and his
invitation sounded more like an order than a request. But, for once, I
was glad to do as I was told and I agreed to meet him after work. He
would come and pick me up that same evening at my flat. And that
was the beginning of a rapid courtship and of one wonderful year in
which I was ecstatically and passionately in love. I stopped living in
my dream-world because the pleasure of living every minute of my
real life was too wonderful to miss. But even in those early days when
I was full of happiness and foolish enough to make plans in my head
for our future together, I could never altogether forego a sense of
unspecified but inevitable doom. Instinctively I was conscious of the
fact that I had to savour and relish this new experience with all
intensity and keen awareness of everything I did.

And seeing Carlo meant continuous excitement, mental
stimulation and a widening of my horizon; it was like being near an
erupting volcano. He was interested in everything. My dull mind was
sharpened by talks about politics and almost convinced that to be
committed to an ideal, as he was, was really the only decent thing a
self-respecting human being should aim at. One day he went
skin-diving off the coast of Sardinia and the next he was off on a
journey across Africa; his interests were wide and eclectic and he
lived alone surrounded by books in a penthouse in the old part of
town. He kept a booklet containing the addresses of the best
restaurants he had visited and prided himself on being a wine
connoisseur. He adored music and had taught himself to play the
cello.

Carlo was extremely kind-hearted, honest and introverted; he
didn't trust anyone and he was neurotically a private person. From
the beginning I knew that he would give me that much of his time and
of his love but no more. Again and again he said to me, ''I don't ask
anything from you because I know that I can't give you all that you
deserve. I can't give you all my devotion. I was made to live alone, to
renounce the joys of having a family because of certain things I feel I
was born to do. I must be free.''

Looking into his dark troubled eyes I knew that he was telling me
the truth—his truth—but, somehow, I also knew that he really loved
me. I kept hoping that one day he might find a firm place in his life for
me; after all, he did spend all his free time with me and he could be
extremely jealous and possessive.

Carlo was never on time as he couldn't squeeze all he wanted to do into a mere twenty-four hours, and he had a chronic problem with sleep. So much did he suffer from the lack of rest that he was likely to fall asleep as soon as he sat down, anywhere, especially in a drawing-room! His car had a habit of breaking down, mostly because he forgot or had no time to fill it up with petrol.

His favourite word was self-evident—all sorts of things were self-evident to him if not to other mortals (sometimes I suspected that he didn't consider himself one). He taught me an immense number of things, covering all fields of human relations. The only unforgivable and really outrageous thing about him was his belief in women's inferiority. "It is self-evident that women lack creativity," he would say to me. "How can they then be equal to men?" I always suspected that he said these things mostly to tease me as he obviously enjoyed observing my indignant reaction.

"What you say only proves that even the most free and progressive of men may remain a slave to idiotic prejudices," I would answer him back furiously. But it was also self-evident that I had been lucky in finding such a person interested in me; when one is near a tornado one is not likely to worry about petty and selfish problems!

Carlo loved to wake up very early in the morning and go for long walks around the town when the streets were empty and sleepy and the sky was still dark. Sometimes he would come to my flat and we would walk to the park, hands in our pockets, often without exchanging a word, just happy in each other's company.

But best of all I remember our outings to the seaside, generally along the coast south of Genoa. We both shared a deep love for the sea and Carlo had a boat which he called, rather inconsequently, *Everest*. Often we would go out in it, a strong wind blowing from the north, the sea jumpy and short and Carlo would put his boat hard into it and we would get all wet with spray. We would come back at sunset and, perhaps, stop at a little restaurant owned by a family of fishermen, and eat some delicious fish washed down with local wine. What fun that was!

There was never a routine with Carlo; he hated that. He would disappear for days without ever telling me where he was going or when he would be back. He might suddenly telephone and ask me to meet him that same evening or collect me directly without warning outside my office. I suppose he was basically a very selfish man but I didn't seem to notice this selfishness, taken up as I was by the sheer delight of seeing him again. Apart from any other consideration, it was always more stimulating and interesting to go out with him than with anyone else I knew and it never occurred to me to turn him down.

Laura, after having met him a few times, pronounced him terrific and gave her approval to our friendship. Quite another story was to get him accepted by my parents. In fact they never did. I explained Carlo to them during a third degree which lasted the best part of two hours, after which my mother declared that he must be mad but harmless. Father swung furiously against him accusing him of being *un poco di buono* (a good-for-nothing) to say the least. That was daddy's way of calling him a crook, a swindler, a chap who might do untold harm to his little girl. Both begged me to stop seeing him. An impossible request. I was seeing so little of him already!

But there were some periods in which we were escpecially close when he stayed in town for a whole week. Then we would sit in a café sipping endless cups of hot chocolate and we would talk about ourselves, our strange relationship, our very uncertain future (it was always I who turned the conversation to that particular subject) and it would be quite late before we separated.

Doubtless it was my friendship with him that made me attach so much importance to the perfect union of two human beings. I contemplated discovering the world with him without realising that he had already seen a great chunk of it and probably with someone else; I imagined an existence in which two equal partners would find the meaning of life in fulfilling each other's needs, without taking into consideration his independence and self-sufficiency. I spent all my waking hours thinking about him. Sometimes when he was away, I would walk past his house, gaze up at his window, and stare at his front door in the vague hope that he might suddenly come out.

But recalling those precious months with Carlo I find that they seem to roll into one long happy stretch in which my natural optimism supported my hopes for a future I had never been encouraged to expect.

On the first anniversary of our meeting, Carlo was in a charming mood and kept repeating teasingly, that it was ridiculous that he should feel so moved at the thought of having been attached to a woman for so long. "A little girl," he would often say, "What am I doing with such a little girl?"

Carlo decided to celebrate the event by going up to the top of the statue of the Madonnina of the Duomo and shout down to all the Milanese our love and joy. He also wanted to distract me from the thought that the week after he was going to Brazil and would be away for a few months. To cheer me up he invented some free time we would have once he got back. That was very unlikely because Carlo never took long holidays but as I needed to believe him, I began to make plans in my mind of what we would do. These thoughts of having a holiday together cheered me up and entertained me for a while after he had left. This was just a longer parting than usual, I was telling myself, nothing more than that!

Then, one day, Carlo must have been gone for about three weeks, I found my boss waiting for me in my office. Very gently and with obvious grief he told me that Carlo had been killed in a plane crash. He didn't know yet all the details of the tragedy because the news had just reached his office. I was the first person he had spoken to about it and now he would have to notify Carlo's parents. That is all I remember, and the pain, only the pain, remains vividly when I think back to the days that followed. I wanted to die to rid myself of the pain.

My parents tried to comfort me in any way they could but I knew that not having approved of my attachment to Carlo, sorry as they were for me, they had breathed a sigh of relief. And I was inconsolable, barely going through the motions of living. Not having yet learned how to accept the seeming injustices of life, I was raging against them, it was so horribly unfair.

Unconsciously, trying to ease my pain, I went back to my dream-world. Carlo is not dead, I said to myself, he can't be. He must be lost somewhere in Amazonia, the only survivor of the crash and soon he will be rescued. Or perhaps he was a member of a secret service; it could so easily be, I argued with myself, he had so many activities and was so often abroad, sometimes I didn't even know where. Yes, that must be it. Thus I was raving away at night, lying on my bed, incapable of sleeping. Perhaps even a double-agent who had been discovered and was now hiding, pretending to be dead; soon he would send word to me, some signal perhaps, who knows.

Going to work in the morning I would look around expecting to see a man approaching me and discretely hand me a note from Carlo. But nobody came and my grief seemed to have turned into a sort of continuous depression which nobody and nothing could lift. It took me a tremendous effort to get through a normal day as I felt tired and listless and completely disinterested in my surroundings. There was no relief in the companionship of my young friends; they seemed so immature and silly compared with Carlo.

But misfortunes never come alone says an Italian proverb and, in fact, more was to come. Mother and I had been worried about daddy's worsening health and she had nursed him for many miserable months. In the spring of 1949 he seemed to pick up a little. I spent a long week-end with them and, as my twenty-first birthday fell on that Sunday, we decided to celebrate it at home. Waking up in the morning, I found on my bedside table a rose and a little parcel with a card from daddy: "A Clementina, sorriso della vita." The same phrase he had written almost twenty-one years before on one of my first photographs. In the parcel there was an exquisite brooch which had belonged to my grandmother. It was made in the shape of two hearts, each one surrounded by diamonds. All the rooms were brightened with flowers, mother had prepared a delicious meal with all my favourite dishes and father had insisted on getting up early and going out to buy some whipped cream for the pudding. Everything had been done with a lot of love and care and both tried to be as cheerful as possible to raise my spirits. After lunch I accompanied him to his room so that he could lie down and rest a little. He slowly opened the door and stood in front of it for a moment. The spring sunlight coming through the window framed his tall, straight figure and lit up his white hair. He kissed me lightly on the forehead and said, "I am so very deeply sorry not to be able to give you a better birthday. Sorry more than I can say."

I softly closed the door behind me. At four o'clock, mother sent me in with a cup of tea. I found him sitting in his armchair with a book in his hand and his spectacles on the floor. Thinking that he had fallen asleep while reading, I hesitated for a moment, it seemed a pity to wake him up. Then I shook him gently and called him softly, but he didn't wake up. With him I lost one of the people I had loved most in my life.

Mother was admirable and efficient. She attended to all that had to be done with care and dignity and we buried him in a small graveyard in his beloved Brianza.

After the death of my father I fell ill. Obviously I couldn't take any more grief and in what seemed then an eternity, I sank deeper and deeper into a depression. I wallowed in it. Some helpful souls suggested that I should look around me at the tragedies of other people. "Look," they would say, "Look around you, everybody has his problems, and you are young and your life is in front of you." But I didn't want to contemplate my future, which I was certain would only be bringing more hurt. And the more they pointed out to me the suffering of others, the more it seemed to increase my own gloom. As I didn't know what to say to them nor how to get better, I tried to hide my moods of despair but, in fact, I had a colossal nervous breakdown. I remember thinking obsessively, in self-pity and self-analysis, the same old thoughts day after day.

Depressions, depressions, depressions, when did they start? When will they lift? They have been with me for so long, I can't remember now. Why? So much time has gone by since Carlo died and daddy too. Is it a psychological problem? Are these old hurts never healed? Dark clouds completely obscuring the light—a sense of hurt in the pit of the stomach, an immense fatigue overwhelming any other feeling. Too tired for acting, too tired for thinking, too tired for making yet another effort. The enormous daily effort to hide from others this mood of total negation. Make yourself get up, get dressed, get on with your work. Smile—the greatest effort of them all—*smile*. A little card pinned on the looking-glass on my dressing-table as I had done before. *Smile*. Don't let others suffer from your inadequacy, don't surround yourself with a grey aura, don't let people see how much you suffer. *Smile,* control your nerves, don't raise your voice, don't show irritability, don't cry (crying is bad for your eyes). *Smile,* be grateful for the life which has been given you. Don't you know that life is a wonderful gift, an adventure, a chance to improve yourself. Have courage. *Smile.* Things will change. *Smile.*

This ravaging pain, sometimes dull, sometimes hurting like a raw wound was hardly absent for long. If it left me for a while, it came back unexpectedly, uncalled for, unwanted and with a vengeance.

The dreadful business of living, day in, day out, through the same meaningless gestures and movements . . . couldn't sleep, couldn't eat, couldn't read, couldn't think.

The energy spent in controlling oneself, the waste! The alternative seemed sensible and reasonable; give up the fight, find peace in death.

Tired, so tired. Nerves playing up. I'm going mad, I'm going mad. Oh, God, help me. The thought of God brought tears, a flood of them. Please, please, couldn't anyone help? How could they, anyway? There is no magic formula—only a miracle. But miracles don't happen when one is in despair, miracles need a positive attitude to faith.

A sense of void pervaded everything. Oh, if only I could sleep; never again to wake up to another day. The misery of it all! How could I have changed so much? And the utter loneliness and selfishness of thinking only about oneself. And so the struggle went on, silently and endlessly for months and months.

Eventually, but very gradually and almost unnoticed, my depressed spirits gave way to the other side of my nature. Perhaps it was just the natural, physical reaction of my young body or the innate exuberant side of my temperament which refused to be oppressed for long, but my innate curiosity and my basic attachment to life started to surface and slowly I began to get better.

My mother expressed a wish to go and live in a pension run by nuns near Portofino on the Italian Riviera where she was to stay, on and off, until her death. Years later when I had married and had a home of my own, she would come and spend long periods with me. She died at the age of eighty-two. For a long time she had been in the grip of arteriosclerosis and her mind had slowly deteriorated. A pulmonary complication killed her. I was abroad when she was first taken to a hospital. I rushed to her bedside but I couldn't be sure that she was able to recognise me. I sat there by her side for many hours hoping she might be aware of my presence. She took almost a month to go, fighting every inch of the way. Sitting there, occasionally holding her hand, I thought with a sense of paralysing sadness how tragic it was that in spite of our mutual love, we had never got on together. There she was now, past any possibility of dialogue, a little woman who was my mother, but of whom I knew so little. Suddenly I had realised that as a human being I knew next to nothing of her. Perhaps the generation gap had been too great, perhaps she had been unwilling to share her thoughts with me, perhaps my priorities had been wrong . . . but now she was going away from me, quite unwillingly, holding on to her last bit of strength surrounded by the love of her daughter and of her few remaining friends.

She is buried near my father in a little graveyard in Brianza where I sometimes go to visit them.

Although I was slowly getting out of my depression, I still had some difficulties in coping with life and when my doctor suggested a change of scenery for me, I was ready for it. My very understanding boss suggested a six months course of English in England and I quickly agreed. I took a train ticket to London—one way.

It was a cold, rainy day in December and some of my young friends had come to see me off at the station. I looked down at them from the open window of the train, clutching my passport and ticket in one hand and a travelling bag in the other. I was glad to go, yet more than a little scared. "Come back soon," they said, unconvincingly. It was as if we all felt that it wasn't to be.

Later, as the train was travelling fast through the night, I let my imagination wander, just as I used to do when I was still a teenager. Uncannily, this time I was to be prohetic; I dreamt of cold, foggy days in a northern country and then again of sheiks and vast expanses of desert land. And, in fact, it did all happen that way. I didn't go back to Italy for more than twenty years and I did visit exotic places, living for a long time in the Middle East and Africa.

Chapter Seven

LONDON

London! A new life, a different life! And how the mood in the pages of my diary changed!

Arriving late one evening at Victoria Station, I felt more excited than I could ever remember. I was moving forwards to a future which promised to be full of new and happy experiences. I found myself walking in a strange town where people spoke an incomprehensible language, whose customs and traditions were different from mine, where paradoxically, people smiled more than in my own country. There was a great river with its misty quays half hidden by a cold greenish fog; large avenues and narrow streets where the northern light played a game of subtle shades best remembered in old paintings and, of course, there was the rain. But even the rain couldn't dispel the excitement of living in a foreign country and in England in particular, which seemed to work like magic in melting down the last of my depression. In fact, although there were still some dark days, reading through the pages of that period of my life, a tale of mirth and fun unfolds.

I was quite unprepared for the British, especially of the post-war days. Even when, up in my tree, I had read about them in my history books and I had listened to my father's descriptions of their country, I had never dreamt of finding such an extraordinary race! Other people had told me that they were dull and obsessed with their self-control but, to me, they looked funny, extremely funny in their ways and manners and, perhaps because of this, almost from the beginning I knew that I would grow fond of them.

I had been given some letters of introduction to some people in England. One of them was to Lady Clare who had an unpronounceable surname and lived in a flat just off Victoria Street. She was a remarkable old lady of great charm who had a few paying guests in her house, mostly young relations of her Italian friends. She took me in and that was the beginning of a long happy spell—almost three years—in which, comfortably settled in her place, I set about to learn English and discover England, her people and her idiosyncrasies. At first my vocabulary was very limited which, naturally, cut me off from the natives and I had great difficulty in understanding them.

I remember a conversation at a noisy cocktail party with a man who later turned out to be an art dealer. He tried to convey to me that he had a Botticelli for sale and then went on to make some noises which sounded to me something like: "Do you still have many of them in your own country?" As I had understood bottle of sherry for Botticelli, I politely replied, "Oh, really? How interesting! But, you know, I'm Italian not Spanish and as I don't drink much, I couldn't say." That took a long time to formulate and, by then, mercifully, somebody else joined us and I quickly moved away!

Not long ago I was talking with a friend of mine about those early years in London, when we first met, and he said to me, "You had, as you still have, a peculiarly toned, but unforgettable voice. Anybody would recognise it, even if you tried to muffle it up on the telephone, as you often did, pretending to be somebody else . . . You never failed to swallow the h's from certain words as in hat, hot, hair, etc., nor to add them gratuitously to other words which do not have them like, well, being Hitalian trying 'er best to speak the Henglish language." But, in spite of dropping my h's and misunderstanding many words when I was spoken to, thanks to the kindness of the natives, who were really very helpful, and to those wonderful London Bobbies who so often went out of their way to help me find mine in their huge city, I managed to do a lot and enjoy everything I did.

Thus, little by little, I was broken into the quaintness of English life, and, in the process, I found it terribly amusing watching some of the people around me: the stiff city gentlemen going about under the pale English sun with their umbrellas and bowler hats, the incredibly orderly queues, Lady Clare's huge cook who was also a fervent drummer in the Salvation Army, the couples who spent their Sunday afternoons sitting in their cars round the Serpentine reading their newspapers.

The quaint expressions of this almost epigrammatic language were also the cause of incredulity, astonishment, even bewilderment, as it was the British way of thinking, of seeing life, and sense of values. I particularly remember being struck by the old colonel seriously explaining to me that the British were now in Germany to teach the Germans how to live! Or by the notion that on a particular day, due to thick fog across the Channel, the Continent was cut off; the belief that, no matter where an Englishman might have found himself—in Italy perhaps—he never regarded himself as a foreigner; and the endless discussions about the weather.

Then there was the first piece of conversation I learned with the accepted form of greetings in the peculiar exchange of questions: "How do you do?" "How *do* you do?" "Lovely weather we are having," they would go on. "Oh, yes, lovely," I would answer very doubtfully as it was more a case of being foggy or cold or rainy or windy and some days cold, rainy, windy all in one . . .

And there was the seriousness of the tea ceremony. Tea was so British, so obviously appropriate, traditional and exclusive, that people were surprised to learn that tea was also drunk in Italy. "Do you actually have tea with scones and cucumber sandwiches?" they would ask incredulously. Then there were those extraordinary, really most peculiar types I saw in the tube, in buses or simply walking down Piccadilly—indeed everywhere. Just looking around me was a continuous source of mirth and wonder.

When the language became a little more comprehensible to me, I had to get used to people and situations which I found perfectly normal but which were described as "dreadfully nice, awfully sweet, breathtakingly beautiful, blissful or riveting". Was this really the land of the British understatement?!

By then, another Italian girl had arrived from Rome to stay with us. She was also called Clementina and together we had the greatest fun observing and commenting on the peculiarities of the English upper classes. Lady Clare introduced us into the nuances of the U and Non-U, from the then fashionable and very popular book by Nancy Mitford. Sometimes she would say that so and so was "not quite", meaning not one of us, not one of our sort. All these expressions mystified us at first and we twisted the "quite, quite" into "quack, quack" and then we referred to people as being ducks and non-ducks. How silly one can be!

In spite of our shaky English we made up new words, like "silly bit", as the literal translation from the Italian *pezzo di scemo,* an affectionate insult often thrown to a close friend or a brother.

I remember my joy when I mangaged to understand my first silly pun: "There are two things you can't do. You can't milk chocolate and you can't pea soup." Or my first joke: "Two fleas came out of a cinema and one said to the other, 'Shall we walk or shall we take a dog?' "

If in Italy people shook hands continuously, here they never did but, at least at the parties to which we were invited, they made up for it by kissing each other just once on the cheek. "Hallo, darling," the women would say, kissing the air in the vicinity of my cheek. Men would kiss my cheek and not its vicinity. To our great surprise they even tried to kiss us on the mouth. And if they saw us home they would ask for a goodnight kiss! "I have never been kissed so much in all my life as I have been in such a short time in London," my friend Clementina confided to me, "And to think that these people are supposed to be so cold and stand-offish. What a surprise!" This was a strange place, we were telling each other, but we loved it!

I remember the first impact of the smell of cabbages around London restaurants, the food coupons, the greasy newspapers for wrapping take-away fish and chips; spaghetti in *tins,* the daily dishes of bread and butter pudding prepared by the Salvationist/ cook. But I remember also the first crocuses and daffodils in London parks, the perfect beauty of a summer day in the country, the outstanding performances at the London theatres and, most of all, the kindness of everyone I met. I began to understand a way of life which had been first unknown, then perhaps alien to me, and I stopped laughing at it and began to laugh with it. And I never looked back.

I was well enough to enjoy and appreciate the luck I had had in being sent away from Milan, and the days would blissfully go by without thoughts of my recent past. I went back to see my mother at the seaside town where she was living. For a moment, on seeing her alone, I thought that the hurt I had so carefully buried inside me, would suddenly emerge and engulf me again as I felt a dreadful pang of physical pain in my heart longing for daddy and Carlo. But it was over after a few moments, and I realised that I had in fact, outgrown my past grief for good.

It struck me as miraculous that I had managed to break free from my past and that I was now slowly becoming self-reliant and near the point when I would shed the irresponsibility of adolescence and reluctantly enter the adult world.

It was good to be back in London. I studied hard (Lady Clare managed to make me pronounce all the h's), but had also plenty of time to make new friends. Some of them were Hungarian and Polish refugees, charming and interesting with tales about their lost countries. The Poles tended to be quiet and soulful and they piously gathered outside Brompton Oratory for mass on Sundays, wearing their long overcoats and looking rather unhappy. But the Hungarians were full of fun and always ready to spend their last penny on a horse or a girl-friend or on a bottle of champagne.

Naturally I saw a lot of Italians but also many English young people, because Lady Clare had a great number of grandchildren and they came regularly to visit her, often bringing along some of their friends. Clementina and I were often asked out by them and invited to their country places for the week-end. But how bitterly cold it was in most of their houses in winter!

Many other Italian girls were in London learning English, often sent by their parents to forget an unsuitable suitor and mend a broken heart. They generally loved the change and mended in no time at all. We made up a largish international group and had a lot of fun together. In fact, I couldn't remember when I had more fun!

I knew a few people at the Italian Embassy and had become very friendly with the family of one of them. At some point he needed some extra help in his office and asked me whether I wanted to go and work for him as a kind of assistant to his assistant. I jumped at his offer and one morning I turned up at the embassy trying to ignore the million butterflies in my stomach. I like to think that I was a less disastrous secretary than I had been in Milan. In fact, I had gone a long way in controlling my terrible shyness and, at least, I could dial a number correctly at the first go!

I had been working at the Italian Embassy for about six months when, through the kind interest of my boss, I received, together with other members of the embassy, an invitation or rather a Royal Command to a garden party at Buckingham Palace. What an excitement! I invested a fair share of my salary in a new dress and went for the first time in my life to have my hair done. I tried to look as pretty as possible when my boss and his family called for me to take me there in their car.

It was a lovely summer day and the lawn of the gardens was full
of people mostly from the diplomatic corps but with a large
contingent of British people. Among them was Lady Clare who
presented me to the Queen. The whole royal family was there. I
was charmed and thought that the young Queen looked a lot
prettier in real life than in the newspapers (of course, television
hadn't come into our life yet), that handsome Prince Philip was
just a wee bit short in the legs and that Princess Margaret's eyes
were the loveliest shade of blue in the world.

Some old gentlemen in top hats were walking around rather
pompously and their ladies wore what seemed to me ridiculous
hats and masses of jewellery. Indian women moved by gracefully
in a blaze of sumptuous colourful saris and some Japanese girls
were dressed in silk kimonos. We chatted for a while and then
refreshments were served under large marquees. Well, wasn't it a
nice place to go for a cup of tea!

So life trotted along and the more I got used to living in London
the less I wanted to go back to Milan. I liked my work at the
embassy and, altogether, I led a very interesting existence. To a
keen visitor, London has indeed a lot to offer.

As I only finished work at six o'clock, I often didn't have time to
go home and change before going to a party or a show. The office
entrance of the embassy was just opposite Claridge's Hotel and I
rather shamelessly used its cloak-room as my private changing-
room, quickly making myself presentable to meet my escort in the
foyer!

I lived happily from day to day making no plans for the future. I
had got over Carlo's death but, so far, no other man had taken his
place.

Then one day, through a mutual friend, I met an extraordinarily
good-looking young man. Tall, fair, slim, as young as I was, he had
charming boyish manners and a most beautiful voice. It was Tom.

There was something particularly fetching about him and I liked
him enormously right from the start. He soon began calling me up
and coming to meet me outside my office. He was often late,
sometimes a little vague but always charming. We would go out
and dance to the Edmundo Ross Band, see Peter Ustinov in *The*

Love of Four Colonels, go to a musical like *South Pacific* or *Paint Your Wagon* and do all the things that young people like doing when courting. We had a lot of fun, laughter and teasing.

I remember once jumping off the number 19 bus, at the bus stop in Sloane Street, right into his arms, to the surprise and amusement of the passengers. Or we would pretend to be frightfully rich and eat by candle-light in little restaurants off the King's Road. Often we would walk hand in hand in the parks during the spring, watching the swans, the people in rowing boats, the splash of the yellow of the daffodils and the red clumps of the tulips.

Once when he rested his hand lightly on my shoulder I found myself thinking how nice it would be to go through life with his protecting presence at my side, an ever-present hand which would banish for ever loneliness and fear.

We used to talk about all kinds of things but mostly about a subject which interested us both enormously—ourselves. Other times he would listen patiently to my tales about Milan or he would tell me about his family. He was the oldest and "the bestest", as I used to tell him, of four brothers and had recently joined a firm with business in the Middle East. He was to go there in about six months time.

I soon found myself walking on air. I paid a lot of attention to my looks, particularly to my hair which I washed every other day, and to what I was wearing; every time the telephone rang, I ran to it as if life was at stake; I kept listening again and again to records of love songs and became rather absent-minded in my work. I also realised that if I asked Tom to do something for me, stressing my foreign accent in a particular way and saying "pleeease", the chances were that he would immediately agree to whatever it was. He would spend most of his evenings with me and when once he wanted to take out to a Chinese restaurant an ex-girl-friend of his, I nearly made a tragedy of it! He had talked to me a lot about his friends and in her case he had painted their relationship in the most romantic light. Thinking about it, I was seized by a rare fit of jealousy and stopping to wonder about my feelings for him, I suddenly knew that I could live with him in complete happiness.

In other words we were in love.

It was incredibly good to experience again all the excitement and the moods, to love and be loved! It was a fresh and unspoiled love, romantic and uncomplicated, very different from the passion and the insecurity of my relationship with Carlo. It seemed to me that my life so far had been a sort of preparation for meeting him.

My trust in Tom was complete. He supplied me with a feeling of security which I had never experienced before. He made me feel at peace with myself, fulfilling my most deep-felt longings and engulfing for ever the fact of Carlo's death. At last I belonged entirely to the present.

I liked Tom's attitude to life and people, so simple and straight-forward. Even more, his gentle attitude towards me, which made me feel secure and protected from all evils. I appreciated his love of truth, his honesty, the fact that he frankly admitted not to know all the answers to life; there would be time to find them out together as we went along.

For a while this atmosphere of happiness in which I was slowly sinking had somewhat a precarious basis since Tom would soon be leaving England to go abroad. But on a beautiful day in May he finally proposed saying, as an alternative to "What about it, old girl?" that he had been going around in a daze, often wearing a black and a brown shoe or different coloured socks in his absent-mindedness which was entirely due to too much concentrating on me. Would I stop this confusion by marrying him and make a happy and tidy man out of him? I quickly looked down at his shoes before promising him a much tidier existence!

Then everything moved fast. Tom wanted to go to the Middle East as a married man, taking me along with him. I still remember how I loved to see him radiating happiness and excitement when talking to me about that far-away country where we would begin our married life together.

We decided on an Italian wedding somewhere on the Italian Riviera where my mother was still staying. It was to take place in a little church on a hill in Portofino, a most beautiful village by the sea with pastel pink and green houses and a lovely harbour full of yachts and boats.

I rushed out there to get things ready and soon invitations were sent out, a dressmaker was sewing my white dress and I was riding up and down the coast on a Vespa scooter trying to get all the documents and papers ready on time. The banns were hung outside the church door, the photographer booked and by the time Tom joined me everything was ready.

I remember dazedly awaiting my wedding day, hardly aware of the many responsibilities and difficulties that married life entails. But how good it was to look at my future without fear and uncertainty, to this future which so often had been full of impossible dreams. From now on I would be able to build it up with my own hands and our lives, Tom's and mine, would be something which we would build and improve as we went along.

And in spite of the many years that have gone by, I still remember vividly the little church in its perfect surroundings, full of sunshine and flowers in the September light. And the smiling faces of my friends—so many had come for the ceremony—and of Cesare one of my father's greatest friends, who gave me away. And the moment of panic when we suddenly realised that we needed a wedding ring for Tom and, typically, he had not thought about it. Somebody rushed into a haberdashery and got a curtain ring to use at the church.

Honeymoon: two weeks in the South of France and down to Spain. Love, shyness, passion, doubt, sleep, food, rain, rain, lots of rain. Two young people discovering each other's bodies. St. Raphael, the hotel shaped like a ship on the seaside and the Alsatian owner, kind and apologetic for the foul weather, the small inn where we had to spend a night because it was too late to return to our hotel, and the bad-tempered concierge who wouldn't believe that we were married. "Ils racontent tous la même histoire," she said, noticing my passport still in my maiden name. And then, Barcelona with its monstrous church of the Sacrata Familia, the bullfight, the little restaurant with the flamenco dancers and Tom smiling, Tom laughing, happy: "I love you, darling".

Then back to London and to feverish preparations for Tom's posting to the Middle East when I found myself suddenly and completely in command of any practical decision to be taken; no doubts, no uncertainties, I knew what to do with confidence and serenity.

I felt that I was finally living out my destiny, there was nothing left for me to wish except that this state of bliss might last for ever. Where was then the little spoilt girl who played up to daddy to have her own way? Or the difficult mixed-up adolescent girl in love with the insubstantial, insecure dream of the first real boy-friend? They had all disappeared, evolved in the process of growing into someone quite new, quite different. I was a woman now; I was me.